*THE RESEARCHED
PAPER
SIMPLIFIED*

HarperCollins Simplified Series
THE RESEARCHED PAPER SIMPLIFIED

PETER CARINO
Indiana State University

■ HarperCollins*CollegePublishers*

Senior Editor: Jane Kinney
Development Editor: Leslie Taggart
Project Editor: Cynthia Funkhouser
Design Supervisor: Lucy Krikorian
Cover Design: Kay Petronio
Cover Illustration: Marc Rosenthal
Production Administrator: Linda Murray
Compositor: Compset, Inc.
Printer and Binder: R. R. Donnelley & Sons Company
Cover Printer: The Lehigh Press, Inc.

For permission to use copyrighted material, grateful acknowledgment is made to the copyright holders on p. 142, which is hereby made part of this copyright page.

THE RESEARCHED PAPER SIMPLIFIED

Copyright © 1993 by HarperCollins College Publishers

All rights reserved. Printed in the United States of America. No part of this book may be used or reproduced in any manner whatsoever without written permission, except in the case of brief quotations embodied in critical articles and reviews. For information address HarperCollins College Publishers Inc., 10 E. 53 St., New York, NY 10022.

Library of Congress Cataloging-in-Publication Data

Carino, Peter.
    The researched paper simplified / Peter Carino.
       p.   cm.—(HarperCollins simplified series)
    Includes index.
    ISBN 0-06-501152-X
    1. Report writing. I. Title. II. Series.
LB2369.C355   1993
371.3'028'12—dc20   92-32434
                                                                CIP

Contents

Preface   ix

■ **CHAPTER 1**
WRITING ESSAYS   1
What Is an Essay? The Product   1
  Length   2
  Essays Versus Paragraphs   2
  Essays and the Writer's Purpose   2
  The Audience of an Essay   3
  The Essay Topic   3
  The Essay Thesis   4
Writing an Essay: The Process   5
  Finding a Topic   5
  Using Invention Strategies to Find a Topic   6
  Writing the Thesis Sentence   9
  Keeping Your Audience in Mind   11

Organizing Your Invention Notes   13
Drafting the Essay   13
Revising   15

Essay Strategies   17
Narrating   18
Analyzing a Process   19
Analyzing Causes   21
Comparing and Contrasting   22
Classifying   24
Defining   25
Mixing Strategies   26

Writing Introductions and Conclusions   28
Introductions   28
Conclusions   36

■ **CHAPTER 2**
READING FOR WRITING   41
Active Reading   42
Making Meaning   42
Responding to Meaning   43

Comprehension   43
Frame of Reference and Context   44
Picking Out Main Ideas   45
Handling Words You Do Not Know   51
Annotating Your Texts   58

Reading Speed   61
Skimming   62
Clustering   63

■ **CHAPTER 3**
WRITING FROM SOURCES: THE MECHANICS   65
Types of Sources   65
Books   66
Newspapers   66
Magazines   67

Scholarly Journals 67
Interviews 67
Avoiding Plagiarism 68

Paraphrasing 69
How to Paraphrase 70
Strategies for Using Your Own Words 71
Parenthetical Citation 73

Summarizing 74
Summaries and Your Purpose 74

Using Quotations from Sources 75
Strategies for Quoting 76

Documenting Your Sources 82

Preparing a List of Works Cited 82
A Book with One Author 83
A Book with More Than One Author 83
An Essay in a Book 84
Sources in Magazines 85
Sources in Newspapers 86
Interviews 86

■ **CHAPTER 4**
WRITING THE SINGLE-SOURCE ESSAY 88

Finding the Purpose of the Source 89

Invention and the Single-Source Essay 90
From *The Great Chain of Life,* Joseph Wood Krutch 91
Brainstorming List 92

Finding a Purpose and Thesis in Responding to a Source 94

Organizing and Drafting a Source Essay 95

Organizing and Developing Body Paragraphs 97
The Three-Step Method 97
The Three-Step Method Turned Upside Down 101
Paragraphs Without Reference to the Source 103

Writing an Introduction to a Single-Source Essay 104
Opening Summary and Thesis 104
Adding an Introductory Strategy to the Summary and Thesis 105

Writing a Conclusion to a Single-Source Essay   108
Revising and Editing Checklists   109
  Revising   109
  Editing   110

■ **CHAPTER 5**
WRITING THE MULTIPLE-SOURCE ESSAY   111
Responding to Two Sources   111
  "In Defense of Hunting," John C. Dunlap   112
  Contrasting the Essays for Invention   114
  Finding a Thesis and Organizing Your Draft   116
Responding to Three or More Sources   119
  "Colleges Must Cut Costs, Help Students," Editorial, *USA Today*   120
  "Colleges Must Not Cut Quality to Curb Costs," Sheldon Hackney   121
  "Taypayer Subsidies Help Fuel Tuition Hikes," William J. Bennett   123
  "It's Simply Classical Economics," Dennis O'Brien   124
  Identifying the Issues   125
  Finding Your Thesis and Organizing Your Draft   128
Organizing Body Paragraphs in the Multiple-Source Essay   129
  Responding to Two Sources: The Three-Step Method   130
  Responding to Three Sources: The Four-Step Method   131
  The Source Sandwich   133
Writing an Introduction to a Multiple-Source Essay   134
  Opening Summary   135
  Introductory Strategy and Opening Summary   136
  Introductory Strategy Without Direct Reference to the Sources   137
Writing a Conclusion to a Multiple-Source Essay   138
Revising and Editing Checklists for the Multiple-Source Essay   140
  Revising   140
  Editing   141

Credits   142

Index   143

Preface

The Researched Paper Simplified is designed to prepare beginning students to write various types of researched essays commonly assigned in college. Unlike most research paper guides, *The Researched Paper Simplified* does not limit coverage to the long documented paper based on a large number of sources. Such a paper, commonly taught in freshman composition with the purpose of preparing students to write similar papers in other courses, is usually assigned in upper division courses by which time students have mastered research in their disciplines. While this text prepares students to write longer multiple-source essays, it also shows them how to write shorter essays based on one or two sources — the kind of essays often assigned to undergraduates in courses outside English departments.

The Researched Paper Simplified begins by offering students instruction for writing an essay based on observational research. In the opening chapter, students learn strategies for invention and organization without having to worry about integrating source materials. The basic sense of an essay provided in this chapter prepares students for the instruction in reading and research that follows. A chapter on reading for writing shows students how to understand their sources, and three subsequent chapters provide carefully guided yet flexible instruction applicable to various kinds of researched writing. Step-by-step methods for paraphrasing, summarizing, quoting, synthesizing, and documenting sources simplifies researched essays for the beginning student.

Peter Carino
Indiana State University

CHAPTER 1

Writing Essays

The **essay** is one of the most common writing products of the college writer, in English classes and for other subjects. This chapter defines the essay and emphasizes the process of writing an essay to enable you to produce the finished piece. Before discussing the process, we define the product. After all, to make a pizza you have to know what a pizza is.

■ What Is an Essay? The Product

An essay is a short piece of writing in which the writer purposely presents ideas and information to influence an audience regarding a single topic. We can break down this definition into various elements that contribute to an essay.

Length

When we say that an essay is short, how short is short? An essay could be as short as 250 words. That's about one typed page or two to four handwritten pages, depending on the size of the handwriting. An essay also could run to thousands of words, say forty typed pages. Usually, the essays you write for college classes will run anywhere from one to twenty pages. Don't be alarmed about that twenty-pager. Usually such essays are assigned only in upper-level courses in your major. So by the time you have to write one, you will have plenty of experience as a college writer and also a solid knowledge of the subject area. In a beginning writing class, your essays will probably range from about 200 words to as long as 1000 words (about four typed pages).

Essays Versus Paragraphs

Although an essay is usually thought of as a short piece of writing, it is longer than a paragraph. In fact, unless it is very short, an essay contains more than one paragraph.

If you read newspapers or magazines, you are familiar with the ways paragraphs help you as a reader. They show you when the writer is moving to a new point, and they allow you to rest your eyes a bit as you read. To grasp this point, imagine if this book were written without any breaks for paragraphs. You would have to read line after line without a break for your eyes. You would probably get tired and quit reading. Unless your instructor assigns a short, one-paragraph essay, be sure to divide your essay into paragraphs.

Essays and the Writer's Purpose

What do we mean when we say an essay "purposely" presents the writer's ideas? A writer has a *purpose* for writing. The purpose can be as simple as wanting to inform the reader about how to change a flat tire or as complicated as wanting to change the audience's views on a political issue. Whatever the purpose, the essay presents the writer's ideas on some aspect of real experience. If an essay is well written, you should be able to tell what the writer's purpose is.

The Audience of an Essay

An essay, like most pieces of writing, is written for an audience. The audience will influence what goes into the essay. If you write an essay telling working parents how to choose a day care center, the financial status of the audience is important for you to consider. If the essay is written for low-income parents, you will offer information about free or low-cost centers provided by public and private agencies. If your readers are high-income parents, you probably will spend more time discussing expensive private centers. If your audience includes both high- and low-income parents, you need to include information on all types of centers. After you have had some practice reading essays, you will be able to tell whom the writer has in mind as an audience. If someone read your essay on day care centers and found that it covered only expensive centers, he or she could assume it was written for wealthy people. When an essay is well written, the reader can easily identify the audience for whom it is written.

The Essay Topic

The definition of an essay says that an essay is written on a single **topic**. Simply defined, a topic is part of a larger **subject**. For example, causes of the American Revolution are one topic in the subject area of American history. Track and field is a topic in the larger subject area of sports. Pole vaulting is a topic within the larger subject area of track and field. Essays are a topic in the larger subject area of writing. A subject is general; a topic is more specific.

The topic of an essay focuses on one part of a larger subject. As a result, the topic often determines the length of an essay. The larger the topic, the longer the essay. When a topic is too large for the length of an essay, writers say the topic is too broad. When a topic is too broad, an essay usually ends up being too general to say very much.

Suppose that you were assigned to write an essay of about 500–600 words with the purpose of describing your hometown to your classmates. If you tried to cover the whole town in 500–600 words, you would have to be very general. You might end up with 100 words on the types of housing, another hundred on recreational facilities, another hundred on businesses, and so on. Because the essay would be so general, your town would not sound any different from any other town of the same size. As a result, your audience would not be getting any information about towns the size of yours that they do not already know. Thus, they would gain little from reading the essay, and there would be little purpose in your writing it.

But let's say the assignment were narrowed down to require you to pick one thing about your hometown and to write an essay with the purpose of showing why this thing would make your hometown a good place to visit. Now, your hometown would be your subject, but the one thing you picked to write about would be your topic. For example, you might pick a local park. Because there is not as much to say about a park as there is about a whole town, you could probably write a specific essay in 500–600 words. With your specific details, this park would not sound like any other park, so you would have an easier time showing your audience why the park makes your town worth visiting.

The Essay Thesis

Simply defined, a **thesis** is the main idea of an essay. Many times this idea is stated in one sentence, called the **thesis sentence.** A thesis is not the same as a topic. A topic is the thing you are writing about; a thesis is the point you make about that topic. Deming Park in Terre Haute, Indiana, could be a topic. But to develop a thesis, a writer needs to ask, "What about Deming Park?" Here is one thesis sentence on Deming Park:

> Deming Park is an ideal place for a family picnic.

Here are two more thesis sentences:

> Deming Park provides a variety of facilities for anyone interested in sports.
>
> Deming Park is the most popular park in Terre Haute.

Each of these thesis sentences says something about Deming Park, and each could be developed into an essay by a writer familiar with the park. Finding a thesis is sometimes difficult for beginning writers. When beginners have a topic, they tend to want to write everything they know about it. When they do this, they end up with a paper that either has no point or has so many different points that the audience cannot tell what point the essay is trying to make.

As a written product, an essay should have a topic that can be covered within the length of the essay and a clear thesis that says something about the topic. To ensure that it has both, you must give careful consideration to both the topic and the thesis during the process of writing.

■ Writing an Essay: The Process

In this section, we will discuss the process of writing an essay.

Finding a Topic

College writing assignments can be different from one another. Sometimes a teacher may assign you a topic. For example, an economics teacher might assign an essay asking you to show whether stocks are a good or bad investment during times of inflation. When a teacher assigns such a specific topic, your job is easier because you do not have to start with a broad subject and then find a limited topic.

Sometimes, however, a teacher might give you a broad subject area to write about, and you have to limit the subject to a topic. Consider a class in world politics in which students spend about a third of the semester studying the United Nations. At the end of the unit, the instructor asks them to write a ten-page term paper on some aspect of the United Nations. Given all that they have learned about the United Nations, they cannot say much about the whole organization in ten pages. So from the subject area of the United Nations, one student came up with a topic on the influence of the Soviet Union in the UN, which he was able to cover in fairly specific detail in the ten pages.

In some cases, an instructor will just assign a paper on something covered in the course. In this case, you have to start with a very broad subject area — the whole course — limit that broad area to a smaller subject area that interests you, and then finally limit the smaller subject to a topic. One student was taking a course in black American history and was told to write a five-page essay on any aspect of the course. Beginning with the subject of black history, she limited herself to the life of W. E. B.

DuBois, a black sociologist and writer. She realized, however, that since DuBois had done so much in his life, she could never cover his whole life in five pages. After thinking about the subject of DuBois's life, she finally limited her topic to how DuBois overcame extreme prejudice to become the first black person to earn a degree from Harvard University.

Learning how to limit a topic takes practice and experience. The more you write, though, the easier it becomes. The first thing to keep in mind is that a topic is usually much more specific than a subject area. However, you also have to be careful not to limit your topic so much that you do not have enough to say to produce an essay as long as you want.

Using Invention Strategies to Find a Topic

Invention strategies are ways to find ideas for writing. Here you will see how invention strategies can be used to limit a subject area down to a topic that you can cover in an essay of 500–600 words.

Brainstorming Brainstorming is the process of listing everything about a writing topic that comes to mind. We start with the subject Deming Park and use brainstorming to limit it to one topic. The following is a brainstorming list on Deming Park:

Deming Park	good place to go in nice weather
sports	softball
duck pond	miniature train for kids
swimming pool	picnic facilities
tennis courts	clean and safe
well patrolled	course for Frisbee golf
children's playground	no drinking alcohol
basketball courts	nature trails
first aid station	lots of trees and wooded areas

Some of the items in the list are general, such as sports; some are more specific, such as the miniature train ride for children. If you sorted all of these items out and grouped related items together, you could probably write an essay describing the whole park. However, since you have only 500–600 words to work with, such an essay might still be too general. You might look over the list and discover that you are most interested in the facilities for families. Limiting your audience to families, you can then list the items that would appeal most to them:

good place to go in nice
    weather
miniature train for kids
clean and safe
course for Frisbee golf
children's playground
first aid station
lots of trees and wooded areas

duck pond
swimming pool
well patrolled
picnic facilities
no drinking alcohol
nature trails

You could also have come up with this topic using any of the other invention strategies.

Clustering Clustering is the process of drawing a diagram in which the main topic is circled in the center with lines leading out to related ideas and details. An example of clustering is shown at the top of the next page. To limit your topic, you could choose one of the related ideas and start a new cluster based on it. For example, you could choose "picnic facilities" as your new main topic and find details that relate to it.

The Journalist's Questions Journalists ask questions to find ideas for writing.

Who? All kinds of people, families, people wanting to play sports, picnickers, young couples, groups of teens
What? Go to Deming Park for fun
When? Spring, summer, whenever it is warm
Where? Deming Park, in picnic areas, around duck pond, on sports facilities (tennis and basketball courts, softball diamonds, swimming pool, Frisbee golf course)
Why? To have a good time, to picnic, to exercise
How? Safely, because of rules, park patrols, and first aid

A cluster/web diagram centered on "Deming Park" with the following spokes:
- Sports
- Good place to go in nice weather
- Duck pond
- Miniature train for kids
- Basketball courts
- Swimming pool
- Nature trails
- Lots of trees and wooded areas
- Softball
- Clean and safe
- Picnic facilities
- Tennis courts
- No drinking alcohol
- Children's playground
- Well patrolled
- Course for Frisbee golf
- First aid station

Freewriting Freewriting is the process of writing quickly, putting down all of your ideas on the topic without worrying about spelling, grammar, or the order of your ideas. Here is an example of freewriting about Deming Park.

> Deming Park is one place that makes Terre Haute, Indiana, worth visiting. Especially in the summer. It's good for picnics. There's a lot to do there, play tennis, softball or basketball, or jog. Families go a lot. To have picnics. It's safe and clean because of the park patrol. There's the Frisbee golf course too, which

kids seem to like. Also they are always feeding the ducks or riding on that train. I guess it's a good place for picnics, or playing sports.

Any of the invention strategies could help you explore the broad subject of Deming Park. But, of course, you would then have to limit yourself to one topic with the purpose of addressing a specific audience.

Writing the Thesis Sentence

As discussed earlier, a thesis is the main idea of an essay, and a thesis sentence states that main idea. Once you have the topic, you need to say something about it in a complete sentence. As you write the thesis sentence, you need to make sure you do not slip back into referring to the subject instead of the topic. Suppose, for example, that you wrote the following thesis:

People can have a lot of fun at Deming Park.

Although this sentence is true, it is too general and too broad. The word *people* could refer to anyone who enjoys the park, and *fun* is not specific enough to get across what you want to say about how families enjoy the park. Since you have limited your topic and audience to families, the thesis has to be specific enough to match the topic and address it to the audience.

Going back to your earlier examples of thesis sentences about the park, you might pick this one:

Deming Park is an ideal place for a family picnic.

This sentence does not sound bad, but as you look it over carefully and compare it with your final brainstorming list, you see that the list covers more than picnics. Although the paper will include picnics, it will also cover family recreation, amusements for children, and so on. Your problem is that in stating the thesis you have been too specific; you need to be more general. Perhaps you could change *picnic* to *activities*. This more general word seems a better choice, but as you look it over, it seems

Writing Essays 9

a bit too general because the word *activities* could cover anything that families do together. So you try *outings,* ending up with this thesis:

> Deming Park is an ideal place for family outings.

With this thesis, you have hit the mark. Not only have you specified that you are writing about families, but with the word *outings* you are being general enough to cover everything from picnicking to swimming. Yet the word is specific enough to let the audience know what you mean.

The following summary of the qualities of a good thesis sentence can help you test any thesis sentence you come up with for an essay.

A Thesis Is Limited A thesis is limited according to the topic and the length of the essay. For instance, a short essay of around 500 words needs a very limited thesis:

Too Broad	There are serious objections to grading systems in American colleges and universities.
Limited by Place	There are serious objections to the grading system at State College.
Limited by Number (One Problem)	Many students at State College value grades more than learning.
Limited by Time	In recent years, students at State College have begun to value grades more than learning.

A Thesis Is Neither Too General Nor Too Specific A thesis sentence should be general enough to cover all aspects of the topic, but specific enough to let the reader know exactly what point the writer wants to make. When a thesis sentence is too general, the reader does not quite know what the paper will say about the topic. When a thesis sentence is too specific, it usually contains details that should come later in the essay or that have nothing to do with the writer's purpose and should be cut altogether.

Too General Many students are too concerned with grades.

Too Specific	Many students at State College just cram for tests and don't care what they learn. (Cramming would probably be only one point used to support your thesis).
Just Right	Many students at State College value grades more than learning.

To make sure your thesis is not too general, try to avoid using vague words such as *interesting, bad, neat, unique, great,* and so on. Also, save your details for the body of the paper.

A Thesis Is Argumentative or Demonstrable A thesis should not be an obvious fact that your audience will accept without support. A thesis can be a controversial argument such as a claim that abortion is right or wrong, or it can be a sentence that just needs to be demonstrated for the reader to accept it.

Fact	New York has the largest population of any American city.
Thesis	A person must make at least $50,000 a year in New York to live a middle-class lifestyle.
Fact	My paper will explain the trade of carpentry.
Thesis	Carpentry is a well-paying and fulfilling occupation.
Fact	University A is larger than University B.
Thesis	Students can get just as good an education at University B as they can at University A.

Keeping Your Audience in Mind

In the process of planning your essay, as you use the invention strategies, form a topic, and write a thesis sentence, you need to remember your audience at all times. While you think of your audience throughout the process, you should also spend some time analyzing the audience directly.

When you write essays, you should analyze your audience by answering questions such as:

1. Who is your audience?
    a. What do members of your audience know about the topic?
    b. What references can you assume they will recognize?
    c. What references must you explain?
2. What are your audience's attitudes toward what you are writing?
    a. Are members of the audience most likely to agree?
    b. Are they most likely to disagree?
    c. Are they neutral?
3. How is your audience going to use your writing?
    a. To inform themselves?
    b. To entertain themselves?
    c. To make a decision?
    d. To examine or solve a problem?
    e. To change their behavior?

If you apply these questions to the topic on Deming Park, they can help you to consider the topic more fully. Since the essay was assigned in a writing class, you can assume an audience of classmates. Which of those classmates is your essay directed toward? Those with families? Any who live close enough to the park to visit it for a family outing? What is their attitude toward the topic? Most would probably be neutral to receptive. In other words, you do not have to worry about hostility, but still you need to show the park well enough to convince the audience that it is worth visiting. How is the audience going to use this essay? One way might be to make a decision on whether to visit the park. Given this purpose, the audience would want to know where it is, if there are any costs for activities, if they need to reserve picnic areas in advance, if the park is safe, and so on.

You have now come up with some points that did not appear when you used the invention strategies — for instance, the possibility of costs and reservations. This does not mean you have to add additional sections to the essay. It does mean, however, you have to work the audience's concerns into the sections you already have. For instance, in discussing the picnic areas, you could tell the audience in a brief sentence how to reserve a picnic area — either by arriving early or making reservations if needed.

Do not lose sight of your audience as you write. Spending some time analyzing the audience will help you to keep it in mind, and you will write a better essay.

Organizing Your Invention Notes

Once you have come up with a set of invention notes, formed a topic, written a thesis sentence, and analyzed your audience, you are ready to begin **organizing** your draft. At this point, you should return to your notes and think about the order in which you want to present the material and then group related information together. For instance, in looking over your brainstorming list for the family activities in Deming Park, you could organize the items in a list like this one:

Beauty of the Park
lots of trees and wooded areas
nature trails

Family Recreation
swimming pool
Frisbee golf course

Children's Amusements
feeding ducks in pond
riding the miniature train
playing on the playground

Picnic Facilities
picnic tables
shelters cover most tables
barbecue grills provided

Safe Family Environment
no alcohol allowed
well patrolled
first aid station

From this list you can begin to plan a rough draft. You have to decide in what order you want to put the groups of material. Also, you might find while you are drafting that you want to change the order.

Drafting the Essay

Keeping the Draft Organized As you write the draft of the essay on Deming Park, you should stay aware of the way you are organizing it. The notes on the essay are put into groups. Each group forms a class of items that would appeal to a family wanting to enjoy an outing in a park. You should try to put each class into a separate paragraph or two so that the audience would not have to sort out all the reasons Deming Park is a good place for family outings. For instance, under the class called "Amusements for Children," you might be tempted to discuss the swimming pool because children enjoy it. But since adults also like the pool, it fits better under the class "Recreational Activities" because that class can include adults and teenagers as well as children.

You might find that one or two of the classes could be mixed. Suppose that as you discuss each family activity, you find that you are integrating details about the beauty of the park — the trees and grassy banks around the pond, the rustic logs of the picnic shelters, and so on. In other words, if you refer to the beauty in your discussion of family activities, you would not have to discuss it in a separate section of the essay. Similarly, the points about safety could be worked into each discussion of family activities — the lifeguards at the pool, the patrols in the picnic areas, the tameness of the ducks, and so on. These two items — beauty and safety — could be mixed in because neither of them is a family activity. But the other items would need to be kept in separate classes. A reader would be confused if you jumped from barbecue grills to the swimming pool to the train all in the same paragraph. Organizing the essay carefully is crucial.

Developing the Draft *Developing* the draft means that you include enough information to meet the needs of your audience and to support the claim made in your thesis sentence. Your invention notes would give you a start, but you would need to develop each point in your notes more fully in your draft. You could not, for instance, simply say that Deming Park provides nice picnic shelters where a family can have a barbecue. You would have to be more specific and detailed if you expected the audience to accept your thesis. It would be necessary to tell how to reserve a shelter. It also would be wise to include some details to let the audience know that there are different sizes, ranging from small shelters with only one table, which would be suitable for a small family, to very large ones with up to six tables, which would be suitable for a family reunion. You could then describe what the shelters look like and what kind of barbecue grills are provided.

Also you should try to bring details to life. For instance, it would be pretty dull if you wrote, "There's a pond where children can feed the ducks." Instead you might try, "In the southeast corner of the park, ducks populate a tree-lined pond, often waddling up the grassy banks, where children enjoy feeding them everything from bread to potato chips."

Including details in your draft is important. If you have your topic clearly in mind, you can draft from your invention notes. But if you think you might forget some of your details, you could use any of the invention strategies to develop one of your points further before you write or as you write. If you need details about feeding ducks, for instance, you could make another brainstorming list to come up with the details that are included in the sentence in the previous paragraph, or you could use a more ordered invention strategy, such as the journalist's questions:

Who? Children
What? Feed ducks
Where? On the banks of the pond in the southeast corner of the park
When? Anytime, doesn't matter
Why? For enjoyment
How? Giving the ducks bread, potato chips

You may think at this point that you have gone backward, that when you are supposed to be drafting you are back to invention. That's true. The parts of the writing process often overlap. Even if you do not write notes for each point, as you did with the feeding of the ducks, it will help to have the invention strategies in mind as you draft each point.

Revising

Once you have completed a draft, you need to revise it. The same considerations apply when you revise as when you draft: thesis, audience, organization, development. Consider the following strategies.

Revising the Thesis Sometimes when you complete a draft, you will find that your thesis no longer covers everything you have written. Suppose that, in writing the paper on family outings, you discovered that you spent most of your draft on the swimming pool at Deming Park. If you have enough information on just the pool, you could cut everything else and end up with a thesis that states that Deming Park pool provides a pleasant and safe place for families to swim. This would be a major change — in fact, a change of the whole topic. Sometimes such a change is necessary because no matter how much invention you do, at times you do not discover what really concerns you until you begin drafting. At other times, you might need to make only small adjustments in your thesis, but always reconsider the thesis after you have completed your draft.

Revising for Better Organization If you organize your notes well, you should have a pretty good idea of the way the parts of your draft will fit together. However, when you complete your draft, you might find that paragraphs could be combined, separated, or put in a different order.

You saw how you might integrate the beauty and safety of Deming Park into the sections on family activities. In that sense, you would have been revising while drafting. But you might not have made the discovery until after the draft was complete. Similarly, suppose that, in ordering your notes, you had placed the section on picnic facilities last, thinking that since it was a major attraction of the park you would want the reader to remember it most. In reading the draft suppose you discovered that many of the other activities would be done in relation to picnicking — children feeding ducks as their parents prepare food, swimming or Frisbee golf after eating, and so on. As a result, you would want to discuss the picnicking first to set up the activities that follow.

Revising for Development When you revise the way your essay is developed, you either add information and details or cut them according to your purpose. Your purpose in the park essay is to show the variety of family activities. Suppose on completing the draft you discover that in discussing the swimming pool you left out the fact that there is a water slide in the pool area. Certainly you would want to add such an attraction to your discussion of the pool. On the other hand, suppose that in discussing the miniature train ride for children, most of your paragraph described in detail how authentic the engine looks and sounds. If this description is so long and detailed that the audience would forget the purpose of the essay, you would need to cut out some of the details about the train.

As a beginning writer, you may hate to cut anything because perhaps you fear that you cannot get enough written down to develop an essay. However, if you fully develop the points that support your thesis and meet your audience's needs, you will have no problem cutting unneeded material.

Revising for Your Audience Any revising to improve your essay's thesis, organization, and development is done for the benefit of your audience. In addition, you may need to make other revisions to account for your audience's knowledge of your topic. For instance, you might include the location of Deming Park. You could probably get that into the beginning of your essay even before you state your thesis.

Many times in an essay on a topic with which you are familiar, you refer to things that you know about as if your audience knew about them too, but that's not always true. For example, in reading the brainstorming list about Deming Park, you may not have known what Frisbee golf is. Although many people play the game on courses around the country, Frisbee golf is not exactly the national pastime, and you could not assume that all your readers would be familiar with it. In revising the essay, you should add a brief description of the game if you have not included one while drafting.

Along with making sure the audience is aware of the meaning of your references, remember also to revise any language that does not fit the writing situation. Though written for a writing class, the Deming Park essay could be rather informal because it deals with informal activities. Thus, if in reading your draft you begin to find big words and long sentences, you could try to use more familiar words and shorter sentences to make the essay less formal.

Once you revise the draft, you would write a second draft and begin editing for errors and misspellings. Once you are satisfied, you would type or neatly write the final copy and proofread it once more before turning the essay over to your audience.

■ Essay Strategies

Many **strategies** exist for organizing an essay. These strategies are often identified as patterns of organization in completed essays. You may have heard someone say an essay is an example of narration, process analysis, comparison-contrast, description, classification, or argument. Once an essay is written, we can identify its pattern of organization, and, in doing so, as readers we can better understand the essay.

In writing essays, however, you need to think of these patterns as strategies that you can use in writing essays. You do not usually start out thinking that you are going to write a classification essay or a comparison-contrast essay. Rather, these patterns result from your thoughts about your topic. For example, if your essay on Deming Park contained a section on picnicking, a section on children's amusements, and another on recreation, the essay would be considered an example of classification because you would have broken down the large category of family activities into different classes of activities. In other words, the topic and the way you thought about it during the writing process would have resulted in a classification essay, a pattern you could identify in the finished product.

Narrating

Even though an essay is not a story, when you are **narrating,** you are telling a story. A narrative essay is based on true events and also contains your feelings and opinions about those events. Therefore, a narration can be an essay. In narrating, you present the material in your essay in **chronological** order, that is, according to the order of time.

If you were to use narration to develop an essay on family activities at Deming Park, you could tell the story of one family's day at the park. You could use your own family or a typical family. You would ask what the family does first, second, third, and so on until you have covered all that the family does from the time it arrives until the time it leaves. For this narrative essay, your notes from the brainstorming list might look like this:

arrives and chooses picnic area
unpacks food and sets up at table
while Dad starts fire, Mom and kids go to duck pond
family eats
whole family goes swimming
after swimming, family returns to picnic area and eats the last hot
    dogs and hamburgers
family begins to pack up to leave
horsing around child slams finger in cooler top and is taken to first
    aid station
family leaves

As you draft this essay, you would follow your list, adding details; but the point is that you would follow the family hour by hour through the outing at the park. This essay would certainly be different from the version that classified family activities.

Which essay would be better, the classification or narration? The strategy you choose for organizing your paper depends on your purpose. You determined that your purpose in this essay was to show one place that makes the town worth visiting. Part of that purpose is to show all the features of the park that would interest families. In classifying the features, you would be able to cover them all. In narrating, you would be limited to what the family did on one particular outing, and they might not have used all the facilities. For instance, the family in the preceding list did not use the Frisbee golf course or put the small children on the miniature train. Both of these features were covered when you grouped family activities into classes.

This does not mean that classifying is always a better strategy for organization than narrating. Many topics lend themselves to narrating. For example, suppose a science professor asked you to write a report on an experiment you did. Your purpose would be to show how you did the experiment and what its results were. In this case, you could use narration to take your audience, the professor, through each step in the experiment.

Analyzing a Process

Analyzing a process, like narration, uses chronological order. In analyzing a process, you organize your topic step by step. There are two types of process analysis. In one, commonly called the "how-to" essay, a writer tells a reader how to perform some task, such as changing a tire, making bread, tying a knot, swinging a golf club, and so on. In this type, you assume that your audience is going to perform the task you are writing about. In the second type, the writer shows how something is or was done. In this type, you assume that your audience is not going to perform the task but wants to know how something works.

The second type of process analysis could help you in certain college papers. For instance, a business professor might ask you to write a paper showing how a company develops and sells a new product. In a political science course, you might be asked to show how laws are made in a certain country. In an electrical engineering course, you might have to write a paper showing the workings of something as simple as a flashlight or as complicated as a computer. In a biology course, you might be asked to show how certain bacteria grow. Analyzing processes is a widely used method of writing because audiences are often interested in how something is done or how something works.

When you analyze a process, you have to consider these questions:

1. What is (or was) needed for the process to occur?
2. What are the steps in the process?
3. Are there smaller processes in the larger process?
4. In what order do the steps occur?
5. How does one step affect other steps?
6. What is the result of the process?

We can apply each of these questions to an essay analyzing how an automobile carburetor works.

What Is Needed? If you are writing about a carburetor, you would have to show what is mixed in it — air and vaporized gasoline — and the parts needed to do the mixing.

What Are the Steps? In the carburetor essay, you would trace the steps in which the parts work to create a mixture of air and vaporized gasoline that is then drawn into the cylinders of the engine.

Are There Smaller Processes in the Larger Process? The way gasoline enters a carburetor is itself a process, which is a step in the larger process of mixing the vaporized gasoline and air.

In What Order Do the Steps Occur? In the carburetor, the air and gas have to enter before they can be mixed together.

How Does One Step Affect Other Steps? Writing about the carburetor, you would have to show how the steps of air and gas entering the carburetor must occur at the same time because it takes both to make the vapor that the engine burns.

What Is the Result of the Process? You would want the reader to know early that a carburetor is a device that produces a combustible vapor to be burned in the cylinders. Likewise, different kinds of writing are the results of the writing process.

Analyzing Causes

Analyzing causes is a very common strategy in writing. Because human beings are naturally curious, we like to know why things happen. If something bad happens, knowing the causes can perhaps help us to prevent it from happening again. If something good occurs, knowing the causes may help us make it happen again. Writing often analyzes causes. An editorial in a newspaper may analyze why the government set a certain policy. College writing also analyzes causes. Consider an essay on why the United States entered World War I or an essay on why an experiment produced certain results.

When do you analyze causes, you start with the result of a chain of events. This result is called the *effect*. You then work backward, looking for the reasons — *causes* — for this effect. A brainstorming list can be helpful. Suppose you are analyzing why a college basketball team had a poor season. Your list might look like this:

star players graduated
poor coaching
tough schedule
newer players lacked teamwork on offense
weak defense
players fought among themselves
injuries

No matter what your topic, you would then have to analyze your causes and divide them into major causes and minor causes. Here is where your judgment comes in. While you might see poor coaching as a major cause of the team's performance, another writer might place less blame on the coach. You also need to explore how one cause might have led to

Writing Essays 21

others. Was the team's weak defense caused by the coach's inability to teach defense or by the players' lack of talent and determination?

In analyzing causes, you must always take care not to simplify your analysis. While you may see coaching as the major cause of the team's poor season, you would have to admit that other causes were beyond the coach's control — players graduating, injuries, and inexperience, for instance. Still, even admitting this, you might want to show that the coach was the major cause. You could organize your causes like this:

Minor Causes	*Major Causes*
star players graduated	poor coaching
tough schedule	no teamwork on offense
injuries	weak defense
	players fighting among themselves

In drafting the essay, you could cover the minor causes first. Next you could argue that even with these problems the team should not have had as bad a season as it did. You could then move to the major causes, and if you wanted to single out the coaching as *the* major cause, you could show how poor coaching led to the lack of teamwork, the poor defense, and the players fighting among themselves.

One way to grasp the process by which causes are analyzed is to remember that an essay that analyzes causes usually has a thesis that is argumentative. In contrast, an essay analyzing processes usually has a thesis that needs only to be demonstrated.

Comparing and Contrasting

Comparing and contrasting is a strategy you use all the time in your thinking. In comparing and contrasting things, you come to know them, and thus you can make judgments and form opinions about them. If you are buying a sweater, you might find two that you like and compare them at the same price while contrasting the color. You compare and contrast people, places, books, classes, TV shows — the list is endless.

Because comparing and contrasting is so basic to the way we think, it is also a very common type of writing, both in college and in the workplace. An executive writes a report comparing last year's sales figures with this year's; a student writes a research essay comparing the early years of U.S. involvement in Vietnam with the U.S. presence in Latin America.

Like all strategies for organization, comparing and contrasting is the result of the writer's purpose. You do not need to compare and contrast Deming Park with other parks because you want to show only its attractions. But suppose you are majoring in recreational studies and are asked to write a paper showing what makes a good park and what makes a bad park. Given this purpose, you could compare and contrast Deming Park with a less attractive park.

If you have a topic that requires you to compare and contrast, you can organize your draft in two different ways: successive coverage and alternating coverage.

Successive Coverage If one thing succeeds another, it follows another. In comparing and contrasting using successive coverage, you would make all your points about one thing and then all your points about another. Notes for an essay comparing and contrasting two parks — say, Deming Park and Fairbanks Park, also in Terre Haute — might look like this:

Deming Park	*Fairbanks Park*
sports facilities	sports facilities
family facilities	family facilities
natural beauty	natural beauty

As you draft this essay, you would first cover all the points about Deming Park before covering the same points in the same order about Fairbanks Park. Successive coverage works well when you do not have many points of comparison and contrast and when your essay will be relatively short.

If you have a lot of points to compare and contrast, successive coverage will not work well because the reader will have to remember everything about the first item in the essay while reading about the second much later. When you have many points, alternating coverage works better.

Alternating Coverage As the name implies, when you use alternating coverage, you alternate between the items you are comparing and contrasting. Rather than presenting all the information about one and then all about the other, you list the points of comparison and contrast and then alternately discuss each item that you are comparing. Your notes for an essay on the parks might look like this:

Sports Facilities
Deming Park
Fairbanks Park

Family Facilities
Deming Park
Fairbanks Park

Natural Beauty
Deming Park
Fairbanks Park

Using alternate coverage, you could discuss as many points as you wanted without worrying that the reader has forgotten what you said about one of the items being compared and contrasted. Thus, you could use alternating coverage for longer essays that compare and contrast.

Classifying

As you worked through the essay on family outings in Deming Park, you got some experience in **classifying.** The final divisions in the planning of that essay, as you remember, classified the types of activities that would interest families. As the name suggests, in classifying, you divide items into classes or groups. To set up a system of classification, you need at least three groups. The items in each group should share some quality that places them in that group, but they do not have to be exactly the same. For instance, if you have a dresser with socks in one drawer, underwear in another, and sweaters in another, you have a classification system. But within one class, say the sock drawer, the items can have differences.

Human beings classify constantly. Like comparing and contrasting, classifying is a way of thinking. It is a way of putting things in order and of seeing differences between one group and others.

Because people often think in terms of classification, they often write the same way. In classifying, the writer usually wants the reader to see the differences between classes for some purpose. In the essay on Deming

Park, by classifying the types of family activities, you could show a variety that could appeal to different families.

Classifying occurs primarily in two ways: according to built-in qualities and according to imposed qualities. When you classify by built-in qualities, the differences in the groups are already there. For instance, if you group teachers according to the courses they teach, you would use the built-in classes of math teachers, English teachers, history teachers, science teachers, and so on. But if you group teachers as good teachers, average teachers, and poor teachers, you would be imposing the qualities on each class. In other words, your judgments would form the classes.

Sometimes an essay can use both systems. If you classify automobiles according to the country where they are produced, you might come up with the following classes: American cars, Japanese cars, German cars, Italian cars, and British cars. Then once you have these classes, you can divide each class by imposing qualities on the cars in it. For each class, your divisions might then look like this: American cars you like, American cars you consider average, American cars you do not like.

You might end up with classes within a class. That can happen, too. Suppose you had a drawer full of sweaters. They form one class of your clothes. Then suppose you put heavy sweaters on the left side of the drawer, medium-weight sweaters in the middle, and lightweight sweaters on the left. You would be classifying items that are part of the larger class, sweaters.

Defining

Sometimes the purpose of an essay is to provide the audience with a definition. When AIDS first burst into the forefront of the news several years ago, many news magazine articles appeared that defined the disease. However, it is more common for **defining** to be used as part of an essay. Analyzing a process, you might have to define a term so that the audience can follow your analysis. If you are analyzing how a carburetor works for an audience unfamiliar with auto mechanics, you would have to define the parts of the carburetor, or your analysis would mean little to the audience.

In defining, your first step is to place a thing in its class. For example, wool is a natural fiber. Your second step is to show how the thing differs from other members of that class: wool is a natural fiber that comes from sheep. You can also add the function of the thing: wool is a natural fiber that comes from sheep and is often used for making clothing and blankets. You can also define by comparison: wool is a natural fiber about the same weight as alpaca. Or by contrast: wool is a natural fiber that is heavier than cotton.

As you can see, the strategies overlap. Your purpose was to define wool, and in defining it you compared and contrasted it with other fibers. Definitions can be as short as one sentence, as in the previous paragraph, or they can be extended, as in the following paragraph.

> Frisbee golf is a game played on a grassy course similar to a golf course. But instead of using golf clubs to hit a ball into a hole, players throw a Frisbee with the object of landing it in a chain net mounted on a pole about four feet high. The distance to the net on a Frisbee course is anywhere from 25 to 100 yards, in contrast to the 100- to 500-yard distances between the tees and holes on a regular golf course. Frisbee golfers begin each "hole" with a long toss, attempting to get as close to the net as possible. Depending on where the first toss lands, players then make one or more short tosses until they land the Frisbee in the net. Scoring is the same as in golf; the player with the lowest number of tosses wins.

The primary purpose of this paragraph is to define. The paragraph starts by placing Frisbee golf in the class of game and then compares and contrasts it with regular golf. The definition also includes some analysis of the way the game is played.

In college, you may sometimes be asked to write fully developed definitions. But rarely would you write a whole essay that is only definition; if you did, you would need the other strategies for organization. While the other strategies enable you to define, remember that short definitions may be necessary when you write essays using the other strategies.

Mixing Strategies

If you read an essay, you can often identify the organizing strategy that the writer has used. At times, however, you can see more than one strategy. In analyzing causes, a writer might compare and contrast one cause with another. Or an essay using any of the strategies might stop to define something for the reader. Sometimes, though, one strategy will clearly dominate the essay, and you will be able to identify the essay by the strategy it uses. Thus, people sometimes speak of a classification essay or a definition essay or a process analysis.

In contrast, many essays will use two or more strategies within the same essay. This does not mean that the essay lacks organization but that the subject requires the writer to think about it and present it in many ways. Examine the following two paragraphs on home computers.

> The two most popular types of personal computers are those using floppy diskettes and those with hard diskettes. The floppy diskettes, as the name implies, are flat, flexible 5¼" squares with a hole in the center. They look something like a 45-rpm record in its jacket, though the jacket of the floppy diskette is soft plastic that cannot be removed. The smaller, hard diskettes are 3½" squares, feel like hard plastic, and are covered with a smooth substance that looks like stretched tin foil.
>
> Computers using floppy diskettes have become very popular, but the computer industry is promoting the smaller hard diskettes. When Apple introduced the revolutionary Macintosh computer, it used the hard diskettes. Following the Macintosh, IBM introduced hard diskette systems, and industry analysts predicted that the floppy diskette would soon be obsolete. These predictions seemed true when nearly all the new laptop computers came out with the hard diskettes. However, since so many people already own machines that use the floppy diskettes, they remain widely used today.

In the first paragraph, the writer is comparing and contrasting the two types of diskettes by how they look and feel. In the second paragraph the writer shifts to narration to show how the hard diskette was introduced to replace the floppy. The purpose of the whole essay might be to compare and contrast the two diskettes; in the third paragraph, the essay might shift back to comparing and contrasting the two on the basis of how much data they hold, or it could include a process analysis on how each one works. The writer's purpose may require many strategies to complete the overall strategy of comparing and contrasting.

It is important to remember that the strategies are ways of thinking. During invention, the writer of the two paragraphs probably thought about what each diskette looked like, how each was introduced, the advantages and disadvantages of each, and so on. This range of thinking led to the mixed organization.

Though we can identify the strategies as organizational patterns in the writing, if you think of the strategies only in this way, they become products. To use the strategies as you write, you must focus on them as thinking processes and remember that the topic and your purpose determine what strategy you use. Sometimes you need not even be aware that you are using a strategy. If you direct a stranger how to get somewhere in your hometown, you do not stop and say to yourself, "My topic is getting to point B, so I will analyze the process of traveling from point A to point B." Rather, your mind automatically thinks in terms of process because of your purpose and your audience's need.

Sometimes your topic and purpose in writing are not so clear-cut. During invention and drafting, you may discover that your purpose requires you to approach the topic using one or more of the strategies; or during revision, if you find that your draft reflects a certain strategy, you can apply it more carefully.

■ Writing Introductions and Conclusions

In a relatively short essay, a paragraph called an **introductory paragraph,** or simply an **introduction,** comes before the body paragraphs. Another paragraph, called the **conclusion,** follows the body paragraphs and closes the essay. In longer essays, introductions and conclusions may be two, three, or more paragraphs long. For now, though, you can think of an introduction and a conclusion as one paragraph each. Introductions and conclusions have different purposes than body paragraphs but work together with them to create the overall structure of the essay.

Introductions

How do I prepare the introduction? Many writers have asked themselves this question. And many beginning writers are often so stumped by the question that we will start by discussing how *not* to begin. The weakest introductions discuss the writer's difficulty with the topic or talk directly to the instructor:

> When you assigned us to write about a community problem, I really had trouble because the small town where I live is really nice and we don't have many problems. But then I came up with this idea for the thesis that our town needs a law so that people don't let their dogs run loose.

The problem with this introduction is that it disregards the audience. In fact, for the writer, the instructor is the only audience. Though the instructor may be your reader, you should write as if you are writing to the whole class. Also, the audience is not really interested in the trouble the writer had with the topic. Rather, the audience wants to know about the town and the problem — the topic of the essay.

Another problem occurs in introductions when writers start too far from the topic:

> Since there was medicine, doctors have always tried to help people. Hippocrates in ancient Greece wrote an oath which doctors still take, and in it they swear to help others. Back in the eighteenth and nineteenth centuries, many doctors worked with little or no pay to find cures for diseases. But today's doctors seem to care more about their fees than about their patients.

This writer is on the right track in that she defines her topic in the introductory paragraph, but she needs to begin closer to the issue of her thesis — doctors' attitudes today. Going back to the beginning of medicine does not get her or her readers to the thesis very quickly, and by covering so many years — actually centuries — she ends up with a vague and general opener.

Introductions are not easy to write, but because they provide readers with a first impression of your essay, they are certainly important, and you should take much care in writing them. It is often best to write them last. That way, you know what the body of your paper says and you can make sure that your introduction leads into it effectively. If you do write the introduction first, it is wise to revise it carefully after you have written the body.

But whether you write the introduction before or after the body of the paper, your readers will expect one. You do not just plunge into a hot bath; you get in gradually. Readers like to get into an essay the same way. That's why a paragraph to introduce your topic and set up your thesis will add to the effectiveness of your essay.

Introductions serve four purposes:

1. To get readers' attention
2. To move readers into your essay while showing what you are writing about before you state the thesis, which is the essay's main idea, or topic
3. To limit your essay by moving from a general discussion of the topic to the specific thesis that your essay will illustrate
4. To state your thesis before moving to the body paragraphs that illustrate it

The following paragraph is a possible introduction for the essay on Deming Park, discussed earlier. To show you how one type of introduction works, each sentence is numbered, and an explanation of its purpose follows.

(1) People who know Terre Haute would not consider the city a vacation spot, or even a place to visit. (2) These people, however, do not realize that the city offers an excellent park system. (3) Perhaps the most attractive park in the system is Deming Park, on the city's east side. (4) During the warm months, people of all types and ages enjoy the park's many facilities. (5) The park is particularly popular with families because *it is an ideal place for family outings*.

1. The first sentence raises the subject area of Terre Haute and the question of the city as a place to visit. Recall that the assignment asked for an essay showing why a particular town would be a good place to visit.
2. This sentence limits the subject to parks in Terre Haute.
3. The third sentence introduces the topic of Deming Park.
4. Here the topic is limited further to people who use the park.
5. The first part of this sentence limits the topic even further, and the second part, which is italicized, is the thesis — what the paper will say about the topic.

This type of introduction is sometimes called a "funnel" because it begins with a wide subject area and gradually narrows down to the limited topic. It starts in a very general way and becomes more specific with each sentence until it finally reaches the specific thesis.

The funnel is a common and effective way to begin an essay, but there are many strategies for writing an introduction. In fact, the number of strategies is limited only by the writer's imagination. Clever writers are always coming up with new ways to begin. Here are a few strategies that students have used effectively. The thesis is italicized in each to show you how the introduction leads to it.

Selecting This strategy begins with a straightforward statement about the subject area. It gives brief but specific examples within the subject area, and the final example becomes the thesis of the paper.

> In the 1980s, the National Football League had many top-notch coaches. Anyone who ever saw a Dallas Cowboys game heard the announcers praising Tom Landry and saw Landry calmly send in the players that led his team to numerous victories. Mike Ditka of the Chicago Bears rebuilt one of the league's worst teams into a Super Bowl champion. Bill Walsh of the San Francisco 49ers, though not as well known as Landry and Ditka, revolutionized the passing game with his multiple-receiver offense. However, *year in and year out, the best coach of the eighties was Don Shula of the Miami Dolphins.*

The opening sentence introduces the subject of the essay as NFL coaches in the eighties and limits it to top-notch coaches. The writer then gives three brief examples of top coaches before introducing his thesis on Don Shula. Note the transitional word *however*. It is used to contrast the thesis and the introductory examples; that is, it *selects* Shula from a group of coaches and limits the essay to him.

Narrating Another way to introduce your thesis is to tell a brief story — to narrate — about you or people you know. In the following introduction, the student uses his experiences on a summer job to set up a thesis about surviving his first semester of college.

Last summer while working construction, I met a lot of guys who were going to college. They knew I would be attending Louisiana State in the fall, so they would always try to impress me by telling me how hard college was. They spoke of really tough tests, hours and hours of homework, and mean professors who cared nothing for their students. I must admit that they had me scared, but now that I have been at Louisiana State for a semester I know that *freshmen can do well if they attend class regularly, don't overdo the social life, take good notes in class, and develop a regular schedule for study.*

Although the student's summer construction job had little to do with his success in college, he used the story of his experience to lead up to the thesis.

Describing Simply describing a person, place, or thing can effectively introduce your thesis.

Person

He was a fairly large man, who always appeared in dark suits that made his cocoa brown skin seem even darker. He had a kind face with a high forehead and sensitive eyes. While he looked like a man with a great capacity for love and understanding, he also projected an image of strength with his sturdy body and determined walk. His voice could be soft and soothing, or it could be powerful enough to rouse thousands of people to action. This man was Martin Luther King, *an American hero whose birthday should be commemorated as a national holiday.*

Place

The room was about twenty by forty feet, with a floor of scuffed linoleum and bare walls of a light indefinite color, which may have been green or blue, or even a sick beige. Leading to the counter at the far end were lines of people, some complaining to each other, others just waiting for the lines to move. This was my first time at the unemployment office. Three months later, I was a regular. *Living without a job means living without self-respect.*

Thing
>   Loops of steel hurtle fifteen stories in the air like the tentacles of some technological monster. Long spines of track zigzag from one loop to the next. It's the "Vortex," King's Island's largest roller coaster, and *riding it is one of life's most exciting two minutes.*

In each introduction, the writer has used specific details to bring the topic to life and set up the thesis. A descriptive introduction can work with more serious topics, such as those in the first two examples, or with an informal topic such as a narrative on riding a roller coaster. Whatever the topic, you need vivid details to get your readers' attention.

Asking Questions   You can usually begin an essay by raising a question or a series of questions. Because a question appeals to the natural curiosity of people, it can be a handy way of getting your readers' attention and introducing the topic.

Single Question
>   If I were to give you an exam from a class you took last year and made good grades in, do you think you could pass it? Many students probably couldn't. These students remember information just long enough to pass a test, but after the test forget most of what they've studied. We are going to college to learn, but I think too many of us just memorize and forget. Everyone wants good grades, but *too many students place grades above learning.*

Series of Questions
>   Do you want to live in the country? Do you want to wake up in the morning to the fresh air and sound of birds? Sound great? Do you want to drink well water that tastes like the pipes which carry it into your home? Do you want to drive five to ten miles to the nearest store for a bag of potato chips? Do you want to haul your weekly garbage another ten miles to the nearest dump? If you still want to live in the country, then you will have to find out for yourself that *country living is not as pleasant as most people think.*

Beginning with questions is fairly easy, but don't overuse the strategy. There's nothing wrong with it, but students sometimes fall back on it too often and thus do not get practice with the other strategies. As you develop as a writer, you should learn to use all the strategies and even come up with some new ones of your own.

Shocking or Surprising Readers This strategy attempts to get readers' attention quickly with the opening statement. The statement can range from mildly surprising to downright shocking. When most people hear something surprising or shocking, they immediately want to hear more.

Surprising Statement

Only a little over half of entering college freshmen ever earn a degree. It is not that freshmen are unintelligent. Young students living away from home may simply get homesick, students who are parents may want more time for their families, and other students may leave for economic reasons. Yet a large number of students do leave for academic reasons. *More of these students would succeed if they took advantage of the help offered by professors and tutorial programs.*

Shocking Statement

Hitler was a hero. Maybe not to people today, but in the 1930s, for many Germans he was the man who was leading Germany back to prosperity and greatness. Of course, these Germans later found out their leader was a monster. We always hear how societies need heroes, but *when taken too far, hero worship destroys both hero and followers.*

In both examples, the first sentence opens the readers' eyes (and ears). In the first, an essay written for freshmen, most readers will want to read on to find out how to avoid becoming one of the many who do not earn a degree. The second introduction comes from a term paper written for a psychology professor. The rest of the paper analyzed how the dynamics of hero worship can be destructive. There was nothing startling about the analysis itself, but you can bet that after the opening sentence, the student had the professor's attention.

Quoting

If you are familiar with a quotation from a famous person or even a well-known celebrity, quoting that person can help move readers into your essay. Readers will quickly identify with widely known quotes, such as John F. Kennedy's "'Ask not what your country can do for you" or Martin Luther King's "I have a dream." If the quotation is not widely known, it will still add authority to your introduction.

> The American philosopher John Dewey once said that the job of the educational system in a democracy is "to teach students how to think, not what to think." Dewey's point, however, is not always upheld in our schools as *teachers sometimes impose their own political and even religious beliefs on unsuspecting students.*

When you use a quotation, be sure that it fits your thesis. In the preceding introduction, the quotation is used as a contrast. Sometimes your thesis might agree with the quotation. If you are arguing that some class does teach students how to think, you could use the quotation from Dewey to lead up to the thesis in praise of the class.

Referring to Something You've Read As a college student, you have been doing a lot of reading. Often your reading can help you begin an essay of your own. In the following paragraph, the writer uses Banesh Hoffman's point about Einstein to set up his own thesis:

> In Banesh Hoffman's essay "Albert Einstein," Hoffman tells how, as a student, he was intimidated by Einstein and afraid to approach him. When Hoffman finally did call on Einstein in his office, he found a kind and simple man who was glad to help him. While all teachers are not as kind as Einstein, *students should not be afraid of calling on teachers during office hours because the students can benefit greatly from individual conferences.*

Referring to something you've read can be an effective introductory strategy. By comparing your thesis to someone else's thesis, you can see your own ideas more clearly. Also, your readers will begin with the impression that you have some authority on the topic because you have read about it. Your reading will support your personal experience.

Conclusions

Just as an essay should begin with an introductory paragraph, it should end with a concluding paragraph, a **conclusion.** And just as introductions can be weak, so can conclusions. As with introductions, avoid discussing your troubles in concluding.

> I have said all I know about why MTV is not harmful to children. I can't think of anything else, but I think my examples prove my point, and I think you should agree.

Like the introduction that gave the writer problems, this conclusion shares the writer's troubles with readers. If the examples did prove the writer's point, they should stand on their own, and he should not be telling his readers to agree.

Another type of weak conclusion lacks development and states the obvious:

> Everyone should get a lot of exercise. Exercise is fun and it makes people live longer, so everyone who is able should have a good program of exercise.

This writer has the right idea in restating her thesis, but the sentences lack punch. They are obviously true, but without development the conclusion is flat and will not leave much of an impression on an audience. Remember that a conclusion is the last thing the audience reads; thus, it should leave a lasting impression.

Purposes of Conclusions Concluding paragraphs have several main purposes:

1. They enable you to stress the importance of the point made by your essay. Often they repeat your thesis, but in different words to emphasize it once more.
2. Conclusions give your essay a sense of completeness so that

readers do not feel that you have dropped the topic abruptly before developing it fully.
3. Conclusions give you one final chance to leave a lasting impression on your readers.

Qualities of Conclusions The most effective conclusions share several characteristics:

1. Often they restate the thesis in different words or imply the thesis.
2. In most cases, they are more general than the body paragraphs.
3. Like introductions, conclusions for short essays (500–700 words) should be fairly short, no more than 100–150 words.

Like the strategies for beginning an essay, the strategies for ending one are limited only by the writer's imagination. Writers are always coming up with new ways to write conclusions. The following are a few strategies that some students have used effectively.

Solving a Problem If your essay has discussed a problem, one easy way to conclude it is to present a way to solve the problem. Sometimes, even if you are not discussing a problem, you can show how your topic is nevertheless a solution to one.

> Without the presidential debates, the voter sees the candidates only in paid political advertisements, which are usually biased, or in brief news footage accompanied by the newscaster's comments. Neither of these allows the voter to hear the candidates addressing issues for any longer than a minute or so. The debates, in contrast, enable the voter to see the candidates, head to head, discussing the important issues. In the debates, the candidates cannot evade questions or sidestep issues without looking foolish. Thus, the debates provide the voter with two hours of unbiased information about the candidates.

The writer of this essay argued that debates during presidential elections are necessary to help voters make an informed choice. In most of the essay, he discussed how debates clarify the candidates' positions on issues, reveal their personalities, and show their ability to think quickly and speak well. In other words, he did not discuss the debates as a problem. Still, in showing how the debates provide a more accurate view of the candidates than news reports and commercials do, he implies that without the debates voters would have a harder time making an informed choice — and that is his thesis.

Challenging Your Readers   Another effective way to conclude is with a challenge, asking your readers to take action or to change the way they think. In the following conclusion, also from an essay on presidential debates, this writer challenged readers to watch the debates.

> Instead of complaining that the debates cut into *L.A. Law* or some other favorite program, we should watch them. We are free to vote for any candidate we please, but if we are responsible citizens, we will make sure that our decision is based on knowledge of the candidates and their ideas. The presidential debates can provide that knowledge, and as conscientious citizens, we owe it to ourselves and our free society to make sure we vote wisely.

Echoing Your Introduction   Sometimes you can conclude a paper by recalling your introduction for your readers. Your conclusion, then, becomes a sort of echo. This strategy works because, along with reminding the reader of your thesis, it gives the essay a kind of wholeness. The writer who introduced his thesis by narrating a story about his construction job concluded his essay this way:

> Next summer I hope to return to my construction job, and if I do, chances are that I will be working with high school graduates preparing for college, as I was last summer. Although I am tempted to scare them just like the guys scared me, I will probably be more honest with them. I will tell them that college is difficult but that students can do well if they work hard and take their courses seriously.

The writer retells the story as it may happen in the future, but this time he is the experienced college student. Note also how the concluding narration leads to a restatement of the thesis in different words.

Looking to the Future Most of the time an essay will cover a topic from the past or in the present. To conclude the essay, you can look ahead to the future, predicting possible outcomes from your topic. The preceding example predicts the writer's future behavior as it echoes his introduction. While echoing the introduction is a nice way to conclude, you do not have to do it in order to look to the future. The following conclusion, for example, came from a research essay discussing the problem of drinking on college campuses.

> As they mature, college students will learn to drink in moderation. If they learn fast enough, they will manage to stay in college while also developing self-confidence in social matters. Others, however, will continue to believe their popularity is equal to the amount of alcohol they consume. Out of these students the most intelligent will make it through college, but they probably won't do as well as they would if they drank less. The less intelligent will eventually flunk out, and they won't leave with a degree. All they will have are memories of the night they won a chugging contest and had to be carried home.

This writer wrote a powerful conclusion. It works well because much of the discussion in the body of her paper supports the predictions she makes. That is crucial. If you use this strategy, make sure that your predictions are within reason. Don't exaggerate, but at the same time don't be afraid to predict possible outcomes of your topic.

Posing Questions Just as you can start an essay with a question or series of questions, you can also conclude an essay this way. (However, if you use questions in your introduction, it is not wise to use the same strategy in your conclusion.) The following examples show variations within this strategy: one uses questions at the beginning of the concluding paragraph, and one uses them at the end.

Questions First
> Why do so many college students drink? Why do they drink so much? Psychologists might say that drinking enables them to overcome their social problems, providing a false sense of confidence. Sociologists might say that students are like the rest

of American society, where per capita alcohol consumption is among the highest in the world. The students themselves might say that they are just trying to find a release from academic pressures. Whatever the reasons, drinking on campuses has reached epidemic proportions.

Question Last

The debates help us to pick the best candidate. We see the candidates under pressure, hear them state their positions on the various issues, and get an idea of their personal leadership qualities. The debates provide so much information that they challenge us to be informed voters. Are we up to that challenge?

Both writers use questions effectively. In each conclusion, the questions enable the writer to emphasize the main point of the essay.

CHAPTER 2

Reading for Writing

Just as writing is a process of making meaning out of experience, reading is also a process of making meaning. Reading can help you to become a good college writer. Studies have shown that students with strong reading skills usually are better writers than students who have trouble reading.

College and most jobs after college require that you develop good reading skills. Even in the short time you have been at college, you probably have had a lot of reading assigned for homework. Perhaps you sometimes think too much reading is assigned, but reading is an important part of learning. Although your professor's lectures and classroom discussions can teach you a great deal, the reading you do in your textbooks will give you the background knowledge you need to understand what goes on in the classroom.

On the job after college, people read all the time. Businesspeople read every day — letters, memos, company reports, articles in magazines and newspapers about business trends. Doctors read studies of new ways to treat patients. Lawyers read law briefs. Engineers read research reports. Actors read scripts. And many of these people, having learned to read well, pick up a book and read for pleasure in the evenings or on weekends. As you can see, reading is a part of life for the college graduate as well as the college student.

Learning to read carefully is the first step to writing essays that respond to sources.

■ Active Reading

People rarely think of reading as an activity. Reading is not, of course, a physical activity like jogging, swimming, cleaning the house, cutting the grass, or even taking a walk. But reading *is* an activity — that is, **active reading** is an *active* process in which the reader must do much of the work.

Students often do not see reading as active. You might think that in reading you sit back passively and just receive the author's meaning as you read. In some ways, this is how you watch television. You don't need to think much because the picture is there before you, and you can hear the words of the actors. You might, for instance, wonder what will happen next in a situation comedy, but you do not have to wonder what a character sounds like or what a room looks like because it is there before your eyes and ears.

Making Meaning

Reading, unlike watching TV, takes concentration and thought. Even though the words are there on the page, you have to put them together to make sense of what the author means. If you are not familiar with the subject of the words the author is using, you ask yourself questions as you read, and you try to predict what the author means. In other words, you fill in with your own experience to try to make sense of the information. In this way, you make meaning. Sometimes the meaning you make might differ from what the author wanted to say. Upon sensing that they do not understand, weak readers give up, while strong readers read the material again.

Responding to Meaning

As you read, the process of making meaning includes your **reading responses,** your feelings about what you understand the author to be saying. You agree with some things you read, you disagree with others, you are confused by others, you confirm and question your beliefs with others. Any questions you ask or opinions you form make up your response. Together with the ideas on the page, your responses contribute to the total meaning of the writing.

Of course, for your responses to be taken seriously, you must understand what you read. Some years ago on the comedy program *Saturday Night Live,* a character named Emily Latella gave opinionated responses to things she read in the newspaper. She never understood what she read, so her responses were very funny. One night she started her response asking, "Why is everyone against violins on television?" She went on and on about how she liked violin music and about how it should be allowed on television. When she was finished, she was told that people were against *violence* on television, not *violins.* She then said, "Never mind." Week after week, Emily ended her act with "Never mind" because after giving her opinion she found that she had not understood what she had read. So while responses are extremely important, they must be based on a clear understanding.

■ Comprehension

Being an active reader helps reading **comprehension.** Simply defined, *comprehension* means "understanding." If you comprehend something, you understand it. That applies to comprehension in reading as well. If your reading comprehension is good, you can make sense of what you read.

Your comprehension differs according to what you are reading. If you are interested in the stock market and know a good deal about it, your comprehension will be high if you are reading the *Wall Street Journal.* If you know little or nothing about sociology, your comprehension will probably be low the first time you read a sociology textbook.

Comprehension is affected by a number of things. Three of the most important are (1) your frame of reference and context, (2) your ability to pick out main ideas, and (3) your ability to understand individual words.

Frame of Reference and Context

Some readings are more difficult than others. When you know a lot about a subject, you refer what you read to the knowledge you already have on the subject; in short, you fit what you read into the frame of reference that you already have. When you have little knowledge of a subject, the context you build while reading becomes your frame of reference.

A **context** is the way things fit together and are related to one another within a subject area. If you can recognize context, you have a frame of reference that enables you to make sense of things. For instance, if you have knowledge of how to do laundry, you know what a rinse cycle is. If a friend said that the rinse cycle was broken on his washing machine, you would refer to your knowledge of doing laundry and know that if your friend tried to use the broken machine, his clothes would come out full of soap. In college, you are learning about many new subjects that you are not familiar with. When material is unfamiliar, you have to try to build a context as you read.

Context is very important to comprehension because a sentence, paragraph, or paragraphs may have a different meaning if read out of context. Politicians often complain that reporters take their remarks out of context. A senator may be quoted as saying, "I want to cut funding for schools." Standing alone, this quotation makes her seem to be against providing money for education, but notice how the meaning of her statement changes in the context of a paragraph.

> I want to cut funding for schools when I see money being wasted on extracurricular frills and trendy new programs that quickly go out of date. But when I see money being spent to reward talented teachers who can make students want to learn or money being spent to provide students with a pleasant learning environment, then I am committed to educational funding.

As you can see, the senator's statement about wanting to cut funding for schools changes completely when it appears in the context of all her remarks.

As a reader, you build context as you read. In reading the first sentence of the senator's statement, for example, you begin to see that the paragraph will be about funding for schools, and at first you may also think that the senator is against school funding. But by the time you reach the end of the paragraph, you have recognized a larger context that shows that she is not against all school funding, just funds for extracurricular activities and trendy programs.

As you write, you always need to make sure that you are providing context for your points. Otherwise, you will leave your reader guessing. As you know, the writing process contains overlapping parts. Some of the overlapping involves reading. To make sure that your writing is supplying the context that your reader needs, you must read and reread your work as you are writing. You can then see if what you have written in one sentence or paragraph makes sense within the context of what you have written before it. Also, by rereading as you write, you can begin to predict what you need to write next. In this way writing itself becomes a means of discovering ideas.

Picking Out Main Ideas

You probably have seen your classmates at times underlining or highlighting sentences in their textbooks. If these students are skilled readers, they were probably marking the main ideas — the thesis and topic sentences. As you know, writers support and develop a main idea with examples. While the examples are needed to help the reader understand the main idea, if the reader cannot tell what the main idea is, then the examples will not make sense. Without the main idea readers also do not have a chance to respond to the writer.

The main idea of a paragraph can be placed at almost any point. It would be impossible to list all the ways in which paragraphs, essays, or textbook chapters state main ideas, but the following are a few common ways.

Main Idea First Stating the main idea first and then following it with specific examples for support is a common pattern of communication. This pattern is often used in speech. For instance, a young woman might say that she is glad she has chosen to go to college and then follow this statement with examples of the career opportunities her education will offer. A sportscaster might say that a certain player is the best in the league and then follow with statistics to support his claim. You use the pattern every day. If you are working and attending college, you might state that it is difficult to do both and then give your listener specific examples of how the hours you spend at work prevent you from studying or how studying late after work makes it difficult to stay alert in an early morning class. More than likely, you have also used this pattern in developing paragraphs in your essays. Professional writers also often begin with a main idea and follow with examples for support. As a reader, you need to be alert to this pattern because if you miss the main idea, the examples that follow may not make much sense. Examine the following paragraph.

> Consider the many hats we expect the President to wear, rapidly switching them like some quick change artist. The President simultaneously is the chief administrator of the entire federal government, the chief diplomat and foreign policy spokesman, the Commander-in-Chief of the Armed Forces, the head of his political party, the key legislative leader, and the shaper of public opinion.
>
> Paul A. Dawson, *American Government*

If you read this paragraph quickly, you will notice all the references to the different roles of the president. However, not one of these examples, by itself, is the main point of the paragraph. It would not be wise to say, for instance, that the main point is that the president is the nation's "key legislative leader." He is, but that role is just one he plays in the context of this paragraph. That one role, however, added to all the other roles, gives us the main idea — that the president plays many different roles — "wears many hats," for the public. Each of the individual roles is one example of this main idea.

As you read your college textbooks, try always to separate main ideas from examples or details because to respond to the reading you need to respond to its main ideas. You know how making your ideas clear helps your reader understand your writing. As a reader, locating the writer's main ideas will make the information clearer to you. When you recognize a main idea beginning a paragraph, you can then respond by judging the examples to see if they convince you to accept the main idea, although the main idea does not always come first.

Main Idea Delayed In the paragraph on presidential roles, the main idea came first. Sometimes, however, one sentence or even two or three sentences are used as a lead-in to set up the main idea in a topic sentence. In reading, you need to be very careful to separate any lead-in sentences from the topic sentence. Read the following paragraph and try to identify the main idea.

> Air conditioning began to spread in industries as a production aid during World War II. Yet only a generation ago a chilled sanctuary during summer's stewing heat was a happy frill that ordinary people sampled only in movie houses. Today most Americans tend to take air conditioning for granted in homes, offices, factories, stores, theaters, shops, studios, schools, hotels, and restaurants. They travel in chilled buses, trains, planes, and private cars. Sporting events once associated with open sky and fresh air are increasingly boxed in and air cooled. Skiing takes place outdoors, but such attractions as tennis, rodeos, football, and, alas, even baseball are now often staged in synthetic climates like those of Houston's Astrodome and New Orleans' Superdome.
>
> Frank Trippett, "The Great American Cooling Machine"

Most of the examples in this paragraph support one claim: "Today most Americans take air conditioning for granted." Notice that two sentences come before this statement. Both give readers an idea of how limited air conditioning was in the past. These sentences can't be the main idea of the paragraph, however, because most of the examples talk about how people use air conditioning *today*. Yet the sentences lead to the topic sentence by providing a contrast to the past.

Main Idea Last When the main idea is stated in a topic sentence at the end of the paragraph, all the examples lead up to it. If you begin reading

Reading for Writing   47

a paragraph and find specific examples, stay alert for the idea at the end, as in the following paragraph.

> The television set casts its magic spell, freezing speech and action, turning the living into silent statues so long as the enchantment lasts. The primary danger of the television screen lies not so much in the behavior it produces — although there is danger there — as in the behavior it prevents: the talks, the games, the family festivities and arguments through which much of the child's learning takes place and through which much of his character is formed. Turning on the television set can turn off the process that turns children into people.
>
> Urie Bronfenbrenner, "Who Cares for America's Children?"

This paragraph begins with examples of the effect of television and discusses the ways in which TV can cast a spell on people and stop them from talking or acting. The paragraph then continues with more examples of what watching TV prevents — family games, talks, arguments — and then introduces the idea that all the examples are what children need to learn to grow up and develop character. Finally, the main idea is stated: that TV can prevent children from participating in the growth process that makes them people.

Unlike the paragraph on presidential roles, this paragraph gradually builds up to its main idea. If you moved the last sentence to the beginning of the paragraph, you would have a paragraph similar to the one on presidential roles. But this writer chose to lead up to the main idea.

When you read this type of paragraph, you need to be careful because sometimes the examples will lead you to accept an idea you do not totally agree with. For example, Bronfenbrenner makes a strong claim against television. Though it may have some effects on children, does it prevent them from becoming people? Is there anything on TV that may help them become people? Raising such questions helps you to evaluate claims that are made as the result of a series of examples.

Main Idea Implied   In the preceding sample paragraphs, the main idea was stated. Sometimes, however, a paragraph may consist of only a group of examples, details, or facts. Together, these imply a main idea without ever stating it in a topic sentence. When an idea is *implied,* it is suggested but never stated directly.

If you have been writing such paragraphs yourself, you are probably familiar with the concept of implication. If not, you still may not be familiar with the words *implied* or *implication*. However, you are familiar with the practice of implying ideas or stating them by implication. On the news you may hear a reporter give several examples of a politician breaking campaign promises. Though the reporter never says so, the examples *imply* that the politician was not honest with the people. Common everyday occurrences often imply ideas. A neat room, a clean car, good grades in school, a regular routine of exercise, and an active social life imply that the person who has these is organized and disciplined. The details and examples of the person's life enable you to make a judgment about him or her. This judgment is an idea implied by examples about the person.

To imply a main idea a writer often needs several examples. You can't imply something strongly with only one example. By itself, having a clean car does not imply that a person is disciplined or organized in general. He or she just may be a car lover and may be sloppy about everything else. But if you add the single example to many others that suggest organization, you imply a general pattern of behavior — a main idea.

Writers often let examples imply the idea. In doing so, they show respect for the intelligence of their audience by not stating a point that is obviously implied. To imply an idea successfully, the writer must have a good knowledge of the audience. If the audience cannot get the main idea from the examples, and the writer does not state the main idea, then communication will fail. However, if the examples do imply the idea effectively, the writer is saved from stating the obvious. Examine the following paragraph.

> Areas that traditionally fall into the province of economists include inflation, taxes, unemployment, international trade, and economic growth and development. More recently, economic analysis has been applied to other areas ranging from marriage and the family to explanations for criminal behavior and war, from aspects of our political and legal systems to questions about environmental quality, discrimination, and professional athletes' salaries.
>
> Ralph T. Byrns and Gerald W. Stone, *Economics*

If you read through this paragraph counting the examples of areas studied by economists, you would find well over a dozen. What does this imply? Well, one implication is the idea that economics is a wide and varied field. Another implication is that because economics deals with many areas, it is a difficult field to define. The writer never states either idea, but the examples imply both.

Main Idea Split A writer often splits the main idea, giving the first half of it in the first sentence and the second half near the end of the paragraph. In a way, this method cuts the topic sentence in half, combining the strategies of main idea first and main idea last. Consider the following paragraph.

> Life is filled with low-level frustrations. Your pencil breaks during an exam, you get stuck in traffic, or you forget to set your alarm clock for an important appointment. To what extent do these minor irritations pile up to become stressors that play havoc with your health? The answer is: to a bigger extent than we imagine.
>
> Philip G. Zimbardo, *Psychology and Life*

The last two sentences of the paragraph complete an idea started in the first sentence. If you were to state the main idea in one sentence, you would take part of the first sentence and parts of the last two. You might discover a sentence like this: Low-level frustrations can cause stress that harms our health more than we imagine. In the paragraph this idea is split by the examples in between.

This type of paragraph is common because it allows a writer to develop an idea gradually, working in examples before the idea is complete. It is particularly common in textbooks because an idea can be related in parts rather than all at once. Also, completing the idea at the end of a paragraph enables the writer to move smoothly into other points. For instance, the preceding sample paragraph, from a psychology textbook, was followed by a discussion of experiments to support the idea developed in the paragraph. Readers need to follow how such an idea develops, to see what the paragraph says as a whole. Therefore, readers must pay attention when new information expands on a point already stated.

Picking out main ideas takes practice, but the more you read, the easier you will be able to find main ideas. Remember that a main idea is just 'that: an idea. Therefore, it must be stated as a complete sentence, just as when you write you state your thesis and topic sentences in complete sentences. In one of the previous examples, the topic or subject of the paragraph was economics. But you could not say that the main idea of that paragraph was economics because economics is not an idea; it is a field of study. To have an idea you must *say something about something else.*

Also, you as a reader cannot respond to just a topic. If someone simply says to you, "Economics," you will probably think he or she is crazy. What about it? But if the person tells you to major in economics because you will make a good salary after graduation, you could respond in a number of ways. The paragraph on economics contains two implied ideas: (1) economics is a wide and varied field, and (2) it is difficult to define economics because it covers many areas.

Once you see the main idea, you can respond. In this case, you might think that because economics covers so many areas, it might be a good field to enter because it offers much to choose from and many job possibilities. Or you might conclude that the writer's definition is not very good because it does not pin down a common point that draws all these areas together under economics.

Handling Words You Do Not Know

While vocabulary building is important to your development both as a reader and as a student, many students often worry too much about coming upon words they don't know. Sometimes a teacher will tell students to read with the dictionary by their sides so that when they come to a word they don't know, they can stop to look up its meaning. This can be helpful for an experienced reader who rarely sees an unknown word and who has a good reading speed. But for someone who reads slowly or often sees unknown words, stopping to look up every word can slow the reader down so much that he or she loses the general meaning of the sentence or paragraph.

The two best ways for a slow reader to deal with unknown words are to try to guess the meaning of the word from the context or to circle the word *after* finishing the sentence or paragraph and look up the circled words in the dictionary after reading the whole essay or chapter.

Guessing from Context   Millions of people have learned countless new words without ever having looked them up in the dictionary. Small children learn new words almost every day, and they learn them from hearing the words spoken in context. This is not meant to discourage you from using your dictionary — it is a valuable tool — but to stress the power of context. Think of all the words you learned throughout your life by hearing them spoken in context. You can learn more words if you pay close attention to context as you read.

Suppose that you were from a non–English-speaking country and you were just learning English. Suppose that you read the following sentence:

> IBM executives were disappointed with decreasing sales this year.

Now assume that you know every word in the sentence except *decreasing*. Could you figure out its meaning? Certainly. You would know that more sales would not disappoint company executives, so you could guess that *decreasing* means "becoming fewer or less." Now read the same sentence with one word changed, and notice how the context gives you clues to what may be an unfamiliar word:

> IBM executives were disappointed by diminishing sales this year.

Just as the context of a sentence can give you the meaning of a word, so can the context of a paragraph. In fact, sometimes you can't guess the meaning of a word from just the context of a sentence. Try guessing the meaning of *purloined* in this sentence from a student essay:

> Just then a clerk grabbed my arm and snatched the *purloined* cap from my head.

If you do not know the meaning of the word, the sentence does not provide much help. But try again, this time using the context of a paragraph:

> When I was nine I learned a lesson I will never forget. All the guys on my block were getting Cubs caps. I had a baseball cap that my mom had brought home for me. It had a silly Little Leaguer sign on it. I hated to wear it around the guys, but my mom thought it was fine and told me I would have to save my own money if I wanted another cap. I didn't have any money, but I had a plan. I went down to the mall on Saturday afternoon

and entered a busy sporting goods store. Trying not to be noticed, I surreptitiously made my way to the back of the store near the caps, and when the nearest salesman was showing some woman some jogging shoes, I put a Cubs hat on my head. I tried to look calm as I walked out the door. I thought I was home free. Just then a clerk grabbed my arm and snatched the purloined cap from my head.

With the sentence in the context of a paragraph, you now can make a pretty good guess about the meaning of *purloined*. What do you know about the cap? (1) It is a Cubs hat. (2) It is new. (3) It is stolen. Since it is unlikely that *purloined* means "Cubs," it has to mean either "new" or "stolen." Either could be the answer, but given that the paragraph begins a story of learning a lesson and proceeds to describe a scene of shoplifting, the word in question probably means "stolen." In fact, it does.

Another word in the paragraph can be guessed from context. The student says he "surreptitiously" went to the back of the store. Although this word is probably too formal for the paragraph, you should try to find out what the writer means. What else do you know about what he was doing in the store? He was planning to shoplift, and he says he was "trying not to be noticed." Given this information, what do you think *surreptitiously* means? "In a sneaky way"? "Quietly"? "Secretly"? If you guessed that the word combines all three meanings, you are catching on.

Guessing from context is helpful, but you can't rely on it totally. A student once wrote a paper on teenage drinking habits. He had read some magazine articles about research studies on teen drinking and used information from them in his paper. But in writing about one of the studies, he said that researchers had found that when the drinking age is twenty-one rather than eighteen there are fewer accidents from drunk driving. However, the study had actually said that the research study *refuted* the idea that a higher drinking age reduces alcohol-related accidents. In error, he had guessed that *refuted* means "proved" when actually it means "showed that an argument is *false*." You can imagine the problem the wrong guess caused in the student's paper. Once you have finished reading, it is wise to use the dictionary to make sure that your guesses are right.

Using a Dictionary If you do not already own a good dictionary, you should buy one to use throughout college and beyond. Avoid small pocket-sized dictionaries. They usually do not contain all the information a good dictionary should. Though you need a good dictionary, you need not spend a fortune to get one. If you can afford a large hardbound dictionary, buy one, but you can also get a good paperback dictionary at a reasonable price. Your instructor may require a particular dictionary for the class. If not, here are a few of the many to choose from. Each is available in paperback.

The American Heritage Dictionary of the English Language
Merriam Webster's Collegiate Dictionary
The Random House Dictionary of the English Language
Webster's New World Dictionary

Although most people use the dictionary to find the meaning or spelling of a word, dictionary definitions can tell you much more. The following is a definition from *The American Heritage Dictionary of the English Language*. All the parts are labeled.

1. Word divided by syllables 2. Pronunciation key 3. Part of speech

4. First definition

5. Examples of usage

6. Other definitions

ef·fect (ĭ-fĕkt′) *n.* **1.** Something brought about by a cause or agent; result: *"Fortunately in England, at any rate, education produces no effect whatsoever."* (Oscar Wilde). **2.** The way in which something acts upon or influences an object: *the effect of a drug on the nervous system.* **3.** The final or comprehensive result; an outcome. **4.** The power or capacity to achieve the desired result; efficacy; influence. **5.** The condition of being in full force or execution; being; realization: *come into effect.* **6. a.** An artistic technique or element that produces a specific impression or supports a general design or intention. Often used in regard to audiovisual techniques: *The effectiveness of the animated cartoon depends on the special effects.* **b.** The impression produced by an artifice or manner of presentation. **7.** The basic meaning or tendency of something said or written; purport: *He said something to that ef-*

7. Idiomatic usage and definitions	*fect.* — **in effect. 1.** In fact; actually. **2.** In essence; virtually. **3.** In active force; in operation. — **take effect.** To become operative; gain active force. — *tr. v.* **1. effected, -fecting, -fects. 1.** To produce as a result; cause to occur; bring about: *"If he is taught to fear and tremble, enough has been effected."* (De Quincey). **2.** To execute; to make: *"important change of ancient custom can only be effected by act of Parliament"* (Winston Churchill). — See Synonyms at **perform.** — See usage note at **affect.** [Middle English, from Old French, from Latin *effectus,* past participle of *efficere,* to accomplish, perform, work out; *ex-,* out + *facere,* to do (see dhe-¹ in Appendix*)] — **ef fect′ er** *n.* — **ef fect′ i ble** *adj.*
8. Second part of speech and definitions	
9. Cross-references	
10. Etymology	
11. Other forms and suffixes	
12. Synonyms and explanations of different meanings	**Synonyms:** *effect, consequence, result,* and *outcome, upshot, sequel, consummation.* These nouns denote occurrences, situations, or conditions that are traceable to something antecedent. An *effect* is that which is produced by the action of an agent or cause and follows it in time immediately or shortly. A *consequence* also follows the action of an agent and is traceable to it, but the relationship between them is less sharply definable and less immediate than that between a cause and its effect. A *result* is....

As you can see, dictionary definitions can tell you a lot. And they can seem complicated! However, all the parts of a definition and the way parts are presented are explained in the introduction at the front of the dictionary. The explanation of the parts of this definition will help you get an idea of how dictionaries work.

1. Word divided by syllables: The entry for each word in a dictionary breaks the word into parts (syllables) according to the way the word is pronounced. Syllables are separated by dots. Paying attention to the syllables can help you spell the word.
2. Pronunciation key: The dictionary gives, in parentheses, the phonetic spelling of the word. That is, the word is spelled and

marked according to the way it is pronounced. Some of the symbols may seem confusing. To find out how to pronounce them, you can check the chart in the front of the dictionary or look at the bottom of the page. Beginning on the bottom of the left-hand page and running across the bottom of the right is a list that uses common words to give examples of the sounds (sometimes the list is just on the bottom of one page). For instance, "âr/c**are**" means the *ar* in a word is pronounced like the *ar* in *care,* rather than like the *ar* in *bar* or *carry.*

3. Part of speech: In the example, *n.* is for noun because *effect* is defined first as a noun. Other abbreviations are *v.* for verb, *adv.* for adverb, *adj.* for adjective, and so on. A complete list of abbreviations is in the front of the dictionary.
4. First definition: The front of the dictionary tells what the order of definitions means. It is important to know because some dictionaries list the definitions beginning with the one most widely used and then moving to the one used least. Other dictionaries arrange the definitions historically, beginning with the way the word was first used and then moving to the more modern uses. In this arrangement, definitions in use today would come last, and the first few definitions might not be in use anymore.
5. Examples of usage: Sometimes, but not always, the definition shows how the word is used in a phrase or sentence. Sometimes the sentence in the example comes from a famous writer, whose name then appears in parentheses.
6. Other definitions: Often a word has more than one definition. Good dictionaries list most or all meanings. Poor dictionaries might only give a few, and you may not find the meaning you need.
7. Idiomatic usage and definitions: An idiom is an expression peculiar to a particular language. A word used idiomatically is used in combination with another word or other words. For instance, the phrase *come over* in "come over for dinner" is an idiom because those words are used together in that way only in the English language. Most languages have idioms of their own. A few common ones in English are *take up, carry on, turn off, sleep in, stay up, wait out.* A good dictionary defines words in idiomatic usage.

56 Comprehension

8. Second part of speech and definitions: Often a word is used as more than one part of speech. The dictionary usually gives definitions first for the part of speech in which the word is most often used. The definition of *effect* first gives definitions of the word as a noun because the word is used most frequently as a noun. Then *effect* is defined as a transitive verb (*tr. v.*). Notice that the definitions start again at number 1 when the word is defined as a different part of speech.
9. Cross-references: Cross-references usually begin with the word *see* and direct you to another part of the dictionary for more information. In the definition of *effect,* one cross-reference tells you to "See usage note at **affect.**" People often confuse the words *effect* and *affect,* so the usage note that appears with the definition of *affect* contains information to help readers avoid that error. Another cross-reference tells you to see the Appendix, a section at the back of the dictionary that tells more about the words.
10. Etymology: The etymology of a word is its history, from its first use to its most recent. The etymology tells you what languages the word came from before it became part of English. Unless you become a language historian, you might not find etymology very useful, but it can be fascinating at times to know where words come from. For instance, the word *sandwich* comes from the Fourth Earl of Sandwich, the eighteenth-century Englishman who invented that particular way of eating food so that he would not have to leave the gambling table to eat his meals.
11. Other forms and suffixes: Suffixes are parts added to the ends of words to change their form or meaning. For example, the *-er* added to the word *farm* to make *farmer* is a suffix. Often dictionary definitions contain suffixes.
12. Synonyms and explanations of different meanings: Words that have similar definitions are called *synonyms.* Some definitions in the dictionary include lists of synonyms, as in the case of *effect.* The synonyms are usually defined and small differences in meaning explained.
13. Labels: The sample definition of *effect* has no labels, but labels are worth knowing about. There are two types of labels. The first type notes specialized uses of a word, that is, the way it is

used in a certain field or activity. For example, under the word *down,* one definition reads, "*Football.* Any of a series of four plays during which a team must advance at least ten yards to retain possession of the ball." This type of label often refers to areas of study from architecture to zoology and tells how people in a given field use the word. It can be helpful because often textbooks use words in specialized ways. The second type of label tells if a meaning is nonstandard, slang, informal, vulgar, poetic (used only in poems), regional (used only in a certain region), obsolete, and so on.

As you can see from the discussion of the *American Heritage* definition of *effect,* a dictionary can give a lot of information about a word. You probably will use the dictionary most to find out the meanings of words, but to find meanings it helps to be at least familiar with the parts of dictionary definitions.

Because a word may have different meanings, you need to be careful when using the dictionary. When you look up a word, you need to find the meaning that fits the context in which the word is used. I remember as a young boy reading a Western story and being puzzled when the book said that some outlaws were trying to rob a stagecoach full of *bullion.* I did not know what *bullion* meant, and when I asked my mother, she told me it was a kind of soup. She was thinking of *bouillon,* which is a broth or clear soup. I became even more confused. Why and how would a stagecoach carry soup? Why would anyone want to steal soup? Finally I looked in the dictionary and found that the word *bullion* refers to gold or silver bars. With the proper definition, things made sense. Just as context alone cannot always give you the meaning of a word, neither can the dictionary. The dictionary gives you meanings. You need to match the proper meaning to the context.

Annotating Your Texts

Annotating your texts means writing in them. The word *annotating* has the word *note* in it. When you annotate, one thing you do is make notes in the margins of your books. You may find it strange to be encouraged to write in your books. In high school, you were probably told never to write in a book. Those books were not yours; they belonged to the school and would have to be used again the next year by another student. Similarly, you should never write in a book borrowed from a library. But since you buy your college textbooks, they are yours, and you can make notes in them as you read.

Even though students own their books, many still do not want to write or make markings in them. Some of these students may be afraid that the college bookstore will not buy the books back at the end of the semester or will give them less for the books if they are not "clean." The cost of a textbook seems like a small sum compared with the hundreds of dollars it costs to take a course. Annotating textbooks helps students learn and understand much more than they normally would. If they are to get the most out of courses that are costing hundreds of dollars, they really should learn to write in their books. As an active reader, you read to understand and make meaning out of what you read.

Annotation can help you (1) understand what you are reading and (2) record your responses to what you read.

Different readers have different methods of annotation. Some use felt-tip highlighters; others use pens or pencils. Readers also may use different kinds of markings and comments. As you become experienced as an active reader, you may develop your own system of annotation. The following is one system to get you started.

Underlining If the main idea is stated in a paragraph, whether it is in the beginning, middle, or end, draw a line under it. If the main idea is stated a second time in the paragraph or stated again in the essay, underline it again. However, avoid too much underlining. When you underline or highlight whole paragraphs, nothing stands out; everything seems important. If a whole paragraph seems important to the essay or chapter you are reading, then draw a line along one side of it. That way the paragraph will stand out in the whole piece of writing, but you still will be able to underline its main point.

Bracketing Often key words or phrases are repeated in a chapter or essay. For instance, the phrase *active reading* was used very often early in this chapter and has been repeated throughout the chapter. The first time key words are mentioned in this book they are printed in bold type to help you remember them. Sometimes textbooks use bold type and sometimes they don't; other kinds of books rarely do. Without the bold type to help, you need to pick out key words and phrases and make them stand out. One way to do this is by drawing brackets around them. Brackets looks like this: [active reading]. To find key words and phrases, look for words that are repeated. You need not use brackets every time, but once you figure out that something is a key word or phrase, bracket it a couple of times so that you will remember it when you see it again.

Making Marginal Notes While you are underlining and bracketing, you should also be making notes in the margins. If you want to make long notes as you read, you will need separate sheets of paper. But the small white spaces of the margins of a book can give you a place to write notes to help you understand and respond to your reading.

One type of **marginal note** is called a *summary note*. This note simply sums up the main idea in a paragraph or section. A summary note for the paragraph that defined economics as a varied field might read simply, "Econ. a varied field." Or stressing how the variety makes economics difficult to define, you might write, "Econ. hard to define." Your summary notes need not be complete sentences, but they should briefly get across the idea you find in the reading.

Another type of marginal note is simply a *question mark*. If you do not understand what an idea means or why a certain example is used, put a question mark next to the sentence.

Question marks can be helpful in two ways. First, sometimes as you read further, your questions will be answered. Then when you look back over what you read, you can often connect your question to an answer. Second, if you have marked a textbook chapter with questions, you can look for answers to those questions in your professor's lecture. If the lecture does not provide the answers, you are ready with specific questions when the professor asks if anyone has questions. If he or she does not ask, you can raise the questions on your own. Do not be afraid to ask. A question will not make you look stupid, as students often think. On the contrary, a question based on the reading will show your professor that you have read the material carefully and are thinking about it.

Another type of marginal note is the simple *yes/no note*. If you agree with an idea, write "yes" in the margin; if you do not agree, write "no." You can also expand on these notes briefly. Of course, not everything you read will cause you to write a yes/no comment, but this type of note is a good way to respond to what you are reading.

A fourth type of note is the *cross-reference*. If you are reading something and the same or a similar idea was also stated earlier in the reading, you can write *cf.* (which stands for *confer,* meaning "compare" in Latin) or *cp.* (which stands for *compare*). After the abbreviation, you can write the page number where the similar or related idea also appears. In addition to the page number, you can add a brief note.

Cross-references are perhaps the most difficult type of notes to make because they require you to think back to other points you read and not just deal with the ideas right in front of you. You should try making cross-reference notes because they will help you grasp the main ideas of whole essays or chapters. When you make cross-references, you are a very active reader because you are pulling ideas together to get to larger ideas.

In annotating what you read, you won't use every method in every paragraph, but try to annotate your reading as much as you can. You will develop better comprehension and be better able to come up with responses. Annotation is work, but it pays off.

■ Reading Speed

The speed of your reading can also affect your ability to make meaning from and comprehend the words on the page. Students who have difficulty understanding what they read usually are reading too slowly. They read word by word. Studies have shown that when reading speed falls below 180 words per minute, comprehension is much lower than at higher rates. Here you will find explanations of two techniques — skimming and clustering — that will help you read faster.

Remember that your goal in increasing reading speed is to increase comprehension, not just to read faster. Remember also that reading speed and comprehension will differ according to your familiarity with the material and the level of difficulty of what you read. Skimming and clustering, the two techniques described here, can improve speed and comprehension if used properly.

Skimming

You can use **skimming** to quickly read something short and simple. College textbooks are not short and simple, as you know. But skimming can help you with college reading if you use it right. That means skimming *before* you read something *carefully*. If you skim material before you actually read it carefully, you pick up some general terms and ideas that can help you improve your speed and comprehension when you do read carefully.

How do you skim? You move your eyes quickly through a line, trying to pick out the key words, the words that give you a sense of what the passage is about. You ignore short words such as *the, a, an, of,* and so on, and words such as *but, when, because,* and the like that connect sentences. Examine the following passage. The key words are underlined.

> In the forties, black writers began to document the effects of the Depression on the people of Harlem. The neighborhood was never to recover from its heavy toll or regain the innocence and optimism of the twenties. By the fifties, however, two towering literary figures, Ralph Ellison and James Baldwin, were to come to grips with Harlem, transmuting it in their writing. Today, again in a period of heightened consciousness, black writers are rediscovering their literary past and attempting to build cultural institutions in Harlem that will survive where those of the twenties did not.
>
> Susan Edmiston and Linda D. Cirino, *Literary New York*

In the following list of the underlined words from the preceding paragraph, you can see how they can give you a general idea of what the paragraph is about.

forties black writers document effects Depression Harlem. neighborhood never to recover regain innocence and optimism twenties. fifties Ralph Ellison and James Baldwin come to grips Harlem their writing. Today period of heightened consciousness black writers rediscovering literary past build cultural institutions in Harlem will survive twenties did not.

Remember that skimming is not a substitute for reading. It can help you only to get the general idea of a chapter or an essay, so that before you read it completely you have some understanding of the context.

Clustering

As you learned in Chapter 1, one type of clustering is an invention strategy involving diagrams. Another type of **clustering** is a technique for reading. In skimming you move quickly through a passage, picking out key words. In clustering, you read all the words, but you group related words together as you read. This method helps you to keep your rate of speed high enough for comprehension. Good readers tend to read words in groups rather than word by word. When people read word by word, they often have trouble understanding because they do not see the sentence as a whole unit of meaning made up of sections. By the time they get to the end of the sentence, they have forgotten what they read at the beginning. You may be used to reading word by word, and you may think that reading a few words at a time will be more difficult. Actually, reading more than one word at a time, after a little practice, makes reading easier. Notice how the groups of words go together in the following sentence: [Our family] [has a picnic] [on my grandfather's farm] [every Fourth of July.] Now read the following paragraph, grouping words set off in brackets.

[Years ago,] [college women] [were sometimes said] [to be studying] [for a MRS. degree,] [meaning they were] [in college] [just to find] [a husband.] [To say] [such a thing] [today] [would not] [only be sexist] [but also inaccurate.] [Young women] [today] [are seriously studying] [for degrees] [in a wide variety] [of majors] [from aviation] [to zoology.]

Reading a paragraph with the words bracketed off in clusters may seem hard at first. After all, in real reading there are no brackets around the words to get in your way. But by reading this way, perhaps you found that clustering makes you train your eyes to see the words in groups. With practice, you will find that clustering helps you read faster as well as understand what you read more easily.

Now try to cluster the words as you read the following paragraph:

> Women had fewer children in the 1970s than in earlier decades. The birthrate, which had peaked at over 3.5 births for every woman of childbearing age in the late 1950s, dropped to less than 2 by the mid-1970s. This trend toward smaller families was related to the great increase in working wives, an increase that was intensified by the economic pressure caused by inflation in the 1970s. Many women who pursued careers put off childbearing, waiting until they had established themselves professionally, while others simply decided to forgo children entirely. The drop in the birthrate also reflected the later age of marriage in the seventies, as well as the ever larger number of single women.
>
> Robert A. Divine et al., *America, Past and Present*

Clustering takes practice. At first you should try it on easy reading material, but if you practice enough and master the technique, it can help you with all but the most difficult reading.

CHAPTER 3

Writing from Sources: The Mechanics

Chapter 1 showed you how to write essays based on personal experience or observation. Knowing how to write essays based on personal experience and observation can be helpful in college, but many of your writing assignments, especially in other courses, will ask you to write about something you have read. The material you have read is called the **source,** and your essay will be a researched essay.

■ Types of Sources

You can use many kinds of sources in your writing, ranging from newspaper articles to books. Before you write researched essays, you should have some idea of the kinds of information that different sources provide.

Books

Books are obviously one type of source. But there are many different types of books, depending on their audience. Most of the books in the bookstores at the local mall are written for a general audience, as are many books in the library. Some books are written for experts and scholars and are more difficult to read but provide very specific information. You will find this type of source more useful as you gain knowledge in your major. Textbooks usually provide basic information on a particular subject and can be used as a source. Also, knowing what is in a textbook can help you understand more difficult sources.

Newspapers

Newspapers contain four types of sources: news articles, features, editorials, and columns. News articles report some event that either has taken place or will take place. They cover news events, such as crime and world affairs. Features provide information on trends, food, people, and so on, rather than reporting a single event. Articles and features do not contain the writer's opinions; they just report the facts to provide readers with information.

In contrast, editorials and columns provide the writer's opinion on something. Editorials appear each day on the same page, aptly called the editorial page, and are usually written by one of the newspaper's editors. Columns are written by people called — what else? — columnists. A column by a particular writer may appear every day or on certain days of the week, and a column may appear in many different newspapers. Columns, like editorials, include the writer's opinion and are actually short essays. You may have heard of or read some of the better-known columnists, such as Mike Royko, Andy Rooney, George Will, and Ellen Goodman. Any of these sources from newspapers can be helpful if they cover the topic you are writing about.

Magazines

There are, of course, many kinds of magazines. Some, such as *Time* and *Newsweek*, report news events. Others include mostly features and are aimed at an audience with a special interest: *Sports Illustrated* for sports fans, *Parents* for parents, *Gentleman's Quarterly* for fashion-conscious men, and so on. Magazine articles can be helpful because they are usually well developed and specific. Because they are written for a general audience, they are not difficult to understand.

Scholarly Journals

Scholarly journals are similar to magazines in that they are published periodically and are paperbound. However, the essays in them are usually written by experts for a very specialized audience. Also, journals are not available at newsstands, as general-interest magazines are; rather, they are purchased by subscription or found in libraries. When you begin to gain a specialist's knowledge in your major, scholarly journals will be useful sources, but for someone with just a basic knowledge of a subject, they can be difficult to understand. Of course, that's how you will learn — by tackling what is difficult to understand — so you should not rule out journals completely. Yet if you find you have difficulty understanding them, don't feel bad; they are written for experts.

Interviews

Unlike the other sources, interviews usually are not printed. But if you are looking for information on a topic, why not ask an expert? Journalists do this all the time, but an interview can also be a good source for a college paper. Suppose that for an economics class you are asked to write a paper on the problems of small businesses. It would be useful and informative to interview some of the owners of small businesses in your town. When you conduct an interview, it is helpful to use a tape recorder if possible because you can't always write down everything a person says, and you won't remember it all. The recording allows you to go back and pick out the most important information.

In writing researched essays, you will be writing about the ideas and opinions of others. But this does not mean that you will merely copy their ideas and present them. A good essay based on sources also will contain your opinions and ideas in response to the ideas and opinions in the sources. Sometimes you might agree with the writer of a source; at other times you might disagree.

Suppose you are taking a class in political science, and you read an essay arguing that American presidents should be able to serve more than two terms. If you disagree with the author, your essay will have to present the ideas given in the essay *and* the reasons that you disagree. If you agree that presidents should be allowed to serve more than two terms, you will have to give *your* reasons along with the author's. Either way, whether you agree or disagree with the source, you need to integrate your own ideas with those in the source. Researched writing, in other words, requires that you respond to the ideas you read. But even though a researched essay requires your response, your ideas mixed in with those of another writer, first you need to learn how to present the other author's ideas in your essay.

Avoiding Plagiarism

Plagiarism can be defined as use of the words or thoughts of another person as if they were your own. In the public sector, plagiarism can result in lawsuits. You may be familiar with a case in the music industry a few years back. A songwriter won a lawsuit against former Beatle George Harrison when the court ruled that Harrison used the music from the song "He's So Fine" in his song "My Sweet Lord." Plagiarism cases also involve words. During the primary elections for the 1988 presidential nominations, Democratic candidate Senator Joseph Biden had to drop out of the race when news media revealed that he had taken phrases and sentences from a speech by a British politician and used them in a speech of his own. These cases show that plagiarism is a serious matter.

Inexperienced writers sometimes think they can copy information from a source into their own essays word for word. That won't work. The words and information belong to the author, and to just copy them and hand them in as if you wrote them is plagiarism. In college, as in the public sector, plagiarism has serious consequences. At the very least, a student who plagiarizes in a paper will receive a failing grade on the assignment or be failed for the course; in some cases, students have been expelled from school for plagiarism.

You *can* use the words and ideas of a source if you do so in the right way. Also, and even more important, when you learn how to present the ideas of a source properly, you learn a lot about those ideas — much more than you would learn from merely copying them. These are the ways to present an author's ideas: *paraphrasing, summarizing, quoting,* and *documenting.*

■ Paraphrasing

Paraphrasing means expressing someone else's ideas in your own words. It is a necessary skill when you write researched essays. In paraphrasing, you need to mention the author's name so that the reader knows you are discussing someone else's ideas, not your own.

To paraphrase properly, it is very important to read carefully and to make sure you understand what you read. You will then present the author's ideas accurately and clearly. One way to build your paraphrasing skills is through *annotation*. As you learned in Chapter 2, annotation means marking parts of a paragraph by underlining key words and sentences and by making notes in the margin.

Read the following paragraphs and notice the annotations.

> What effects does television have on the candidates themselves? It dictates priorities that are different from those of an earlier day. The physical appearance of the candidate is increasingly important. Does he or she look fit, well-rested, secure? Losing candidates like Adlai Stevenson, Hubert Humphrey, and Richard Nixon all seemed to look "bad" on TV. Nixon overcame this problem in 1972 with ads that featured longer shots of him being "presidential" — flying off to China. Close-ups were avoided.
>
> Both John Kennedy and Jimmy Carter seemed more at home with the medium, perhaps because both were youthful, informal,

TV makes looks important
Losers looked bad on TV
Kennedy & Carter looked good: young

> *Eisenhower + Johnson looked fatherly*
>
> physically active outdoor types. Dwight Eisenhower and Lyndon Johnson seemed to have a <u>paternal, fatherly image</u> on the small screen.
>
> E. J. Whetmore, *The Selling of the President*

The notes in the margin condense and restate the sentences that are underlined. The first underlined sentence is the answer to the question Whetmore raises. That is the topic sentence and the main idea of the paragraphs. The underlining and the marginal notes about Whetmore's examples are useful because when the writer paraphrases — puts the paragraphs in his or her own words — he or she will need to show how Whetmore proves his point. The writer can then use the annotations as the basis for a paraphrase of Whetmore's paragraphs. Consider the following paraphrase:

> According to E. J. Whetmore, a presidential candidate's looks are becoming more and more important because of television. On television, voters can see if a candidate is healthy and if he seems secure. Whetmore says that unsuccessful candidates such as Stevenson, Humphrey, and Nixon did not look good on television. When Nixon won in 1972, he avoided close-ups on TV. Whetmore also shows that winning candidates did look good. Kennedy and Carter were young-looking, friendly, and athletic, while Eisenhower and Johnson looked fatherly on TV.

Notice that the paraphrase presents both Whetmore's main idea about the importance of a candidate's appearance on television and the examples Whetmore uses to support his point.

How to Paraphrase

To write a good paraphrase, you need to follow three steps.

Read Carefully Make sure you understand the material you are reading. Separate main ideas from examples, and try to figure out the relationship between them. Annotation can help; use the methods presented in Chapter 2.

Use a Tag A **tag** is a reference to the name of the author who wrote the source. You use a tag so that readers know you are presenting someone else's ideas. In the previous example, Whetmore's name is mentioned: "According to E. J. Whetmore . . ., Whetmore says . . ., Whetmore also shows."

Using a tag is not difficult. You can write "According to _____" or "As _____ says." You can also use the author's name and a verb to lead in to your sentence: "_____ says. . . ." Here is a list of handy verbs that can be used easily with the tag:

argues
asserts
believes
claims
contends
demonstrates

illustrates
offers
says
shows
states

Although using tags may be new to you, you have been using them all your life in everyday conversations. If as a child you said to a friend, "My mom said I can't come out to play," you used a tag. In your conversations with friends now, you use a tag every time you tell one friend something that another friend said. For example, "Pam claimed that she did not know she was supposed to meet me last night." Just for practice, listen to yourself and your friends speak today and try to notice the many times tags are used.

Put the Ideas in Your Own Words While all of these steps are important, this one is probably the most difficult, but the following section gives you steps to help you learn how to put a source's ideas in your words.

Strategies for Using Your Own Words

Often you use your words to retell something that someone else has said. Suppose a friend named Mike tells you about a trip he has taken. Later that day you see another friend who also knows Mike. When you tell the second friend that you talked to Mike earlier, she asks if he said anything about his vacation. You then retell what Mike told you. However, in the retelling, the words you choose and the structure of your sentences will not be the same as Mike's.

A paraphrase is similar, but because the author's words and sentences are there on the page to keep reminding you exactly what the author is saying, putting the information into your own words can be difficult. The following strategies can help.

Change the Sentence Structure Try not to use the same type and order of clauses and phrases that are used in the source you are paraphrasing.

Paraphrase "Blindly" This means to read the whole paragraph (or paragraphs), make notes, and then write a paraphrase without looking back at the material. Paraphrasing blindly will help you to change the sentence structure because you often won't remember the structure of the author's sentences.

Do Not Use More Than Three or Four Consecutive Words of the Source Even when you try to change the sentence structure and use your own words, you will often find that your paraphrase still contains three- or four-word phrases that belong to the author. Unless these are very common phrases — for example, "in the morning" — you should rewrite the words or even the whole sentence.

Use Synonyms A synonym is a word that means approximately the same thing as another word. In the following sentence the words *appeared* and *looked* are synonyms:

> Yesterday morning the patient appeared better, but by evening he looked ill again.

Students who lack experience in paraphrasing often think they can merely replace a few words in a source with synonyms and have a good paraphrase. Synonyms are helpful and should be used, but they are only one step in paraphrasing. Make sure that you follow the other rules for paraphrasing too.

Use Key Words from the Source While you need to paraphrase in your words, you cannot and need not substitute a different word for every word in the original. The paraphrase of Whetmore earlier in this chapter used the words *television* and *presidents*. Because these are common words in the English language and do not belong exclusively to Whetmore, another writer can use them in a paraphrase. To substitute the slang word *tube* for television would be needless and silly. To substitute *chief executives of America* would also be needless and would sound unnatural. Whetmore is writing about television and presidents. Those are his key words, and the paraphrase must use them if it is to present the source clearly.

Do Not Use Striking or Catchy Language   In referring to **striking or catchy language,** we mean that some writers use clever phrases that most people would not think of. For instance, if ten students wrote a paragraph on Michael Jordan, the Chicago Bulls' basketball player, and one student described Jordan as "a whirling dervish in gym shorts," that student would be using striking or catchy language and you could not use those words in a paraphrase.

Striking or catchy language is a group of words that is original and imaginative. Think about your everyday conversations. Just joking around, you often hear people use striking or catchy phrases. Often you repeat them in your own conversation. That's okay because conversation is not published writing. But remember that when you paraphrase, you should not use another author's striking or catchy phrases. If you want to use them, you will need to put quotation marks around them (explained in later sections in this chapter).

Parenthetical Citation

When you paraphrase a source, you need to tell your readers the page from which you have taken the information. **Parenthetical citation** means that you put the page number in parentheses following the material:

> Gideon E. Nelson says that there are two basic reasons why Americans have become strongly diet conscious: health and vanity (52).

Note the page number in parentheses following the last word in the sentence but coming before the period. You should also use parenthetical citation when you are summarizing or quoting sources, two methods covered later in this chapter.

Writing from Sources: The Mechanics   73

■ Summarizing

When you write a paraphrase, you present everything the author says in his or her sentence or paragraph. Paraphrasing can come in handy when all the specific examples are important to the main idea of the source or when you want to show how the author is using the specific examples. But when you write your own essay in response to a source, you cannot paraphrase the whole source. Imagine trying to paraphrase a whole textbook, or even one chapter! Your essay would be as long as the source, you would not have room for your own ideas, and your reader could just as easily read the original source rather than your paper.

Unlike a paraphrase, a **summary** is a short version of the source, presenting only the author's main idea. Because a summary is short, it is also general. As a short version of the source, the summary does *not* present all the specific examples as a paraphrase does. Again, you use summaries all the time in everyday conversations. Suppose you have taken a major examination. After class, you meet a friend and she asks about the exam. Because you don't have time to stop and tell her all about it, you say, "It was tough, but I think I did okay." Your answer is a summary. It gives your friend only a general idea of the exam. Compare this short summary answer to the longer, detailed answer you would give if you were having lunch with a friend who asked to hear all about your exam. Then you would probably tell how long the exam was, what the questions were like, how many questions there were, how long it took you to complete them, and so on. A summary leaves out these specific details. It tells rather than shows.

Basically, when you summarize a paragraph, you pick out the main idea and, using your own words, state it in one or two sentences. When you summarize a whole essay, you begin by stating its thesis and then state the main ideas from sections or paragraphs that support and develop the thesis, all in your own words.

Summaries and Your Purpose

Summaries are always much shorter than the original version. However, summaries can be different lengths depending on your purpose. You can use any of the following strategies to write a summary.

1. Write a one-paragraph or a one-page summary of something you have read for a class, such as a textbook chapter. This kind of summary serves two purposes. First, by summarizing the material, you understand the main points of the source. Second, the summary can help you study when the time comes to be examined on the source.
2. Use a one-paragraph summary in a paper on a source. Your introduction to the paper might summarize the source before you move into a more detailed discussion of the source's points. In a longer paper on more than one source, you might use a one-paragraph summary in the body of your paper to set up a comparison of one source with another.
3. Write a one-sentence summary to show briefly the point of a source before you move to your own points. Such a one-sentence summary is too brief to use for study notes, but it can be very handy when you are writing researched papers.

Whether you are using a one-paragraph or one-sentence summary, remember to cite it with the page number in parentheses.

■ Using Quotations from Sources

In paraphrasing and summarizing, you put the words of a source into your own words. Paraphrasing and summarizing are handy and necessary skills because you learn a great deal by being able to understand a source well enough to put it in your words. Also, when you write papers in college and on the job, you cannot copy a source word for word.

Sometimes, however, you might want to use the original words from a source for one of these reasons:

1. The language is so striking or catchy that you would like to have it preserved in your paper. It would be foolish, for instance, to paraphrase John F. Kennedy's famous statement "Ask not what your country can do for you, ask what you can do for your country." By quoting Kennedy word for word, you allow his language to have the same impact on your reader that it first had on you.

2. The language is too complex to paraphrase. In such a case, you might feel that if you were to paraphrase, you would change the meaning of the source. This problem comes up sometimes when you are working with highly technical material or with a subject that is difficult for you.
3. You want to give the reader a general idea of the language of the source. If you were writing about literature — a poem or a short story — using quotations would give your reader some idea of the style of the writer.

When you quote, you need to remember that the **quotation** must contain the *exact* words of the source. Whatever your reason for quoting a source, you set off the quotation with *quotation marks*. The quotation marks tell your readers that the words between the marks belong to the source.

When quoting, you also need to use tags. You can place a tag before the quote, as in paraphrasing: John F. Kennedy said, "Ask not what your country can do for you, ask what you can do for your country." Or you can place the tag in parentheses after the quotation at the end of your sentence: "Ask not what your country can do for you, ask what you can do for your country" (John F. Kennedy). Also remember to cite the page number in parentheses when you quote, just as you did when paraphrasing and summarizing.

Strategies for Quoting

You can use many strategies for quoting a source in your writing. The following discussions and examples will help you learn to use the different strategies. As you study each strategy, remember that you must use the author's exact words; you must tag the quotation with the author's name, either in the wording of the sentence or in parentheses at the end of the sentence; and you must give the page number, in parentheses, where the quotation comes from in the source.

Quote a Small Piece of the Source in Your Sentence This strategy allows you to include short phrases or sentences that use striking or catchy language or language that it would be too difficult to paraphrase.

Many people get cheated on repairs, and one "gold mine for crooked repairmen" is air-conditioner repair (Purdy, 9).

Holidays aren't what they used to be, yet greeting card companies, as Betty Rollin says, have come up with "an infinite variety of occasions about which to fashion a 50-cent card" (1).

The average person pays his check after eating, but "it would be remarkably easy to wander away from a meal without paying" (Greene, 29).

When you quote a brief part of the source, make sure that it fits into your sentence correctly. Sometimes the use of a quotation can lead to an error in grammar if you are not careful. What is the error in the following sentence?

The average person pays his check after eating "it would be remarkably easy to wander away from a meal without paying" (Greene, 29).

If you could not recognize the error right away, consider that the student's words make up one complete sentence: *The average person pays his check after eating.* And the quotation of author Bob Greene makes up another complete sentence: *"It would be remarkably easy to wander away from a meal without paying."* But the two sentences are run together without punctuation and a connecting word. Thus, the student has written a run-on sentence. If you compare the run-on sentence to the correct example preceding it, you will see that the comma and connecting word *but* allow the two sentences to be joined correctly.

Introduce a Quoted Sentence with a Colon Using a colon is one way to avoid a run-on sentence when you are joining your sentence to a sentence from a source. Aside from helping you avoid an error, the colon is a useful strategy for quoting a source. Study the following examples:

The punishment a man absorbs in a boxing ring is not always evident while the fight is taking place: "A prizefighter may be able to survive even repeated brain concussions, but the damage to his brain may be permanent" (Smith, 11).

> Jane E. Brody argues that marijuana has various effects on the brain: "a marijuana high impairs memory, learning, speech, reading comprehension, arithmetic problem-solving and the ability to think" (16).

The colon allows you to state a point and then support it with a quotation. When you use a colon, you must have a complete sentence before it.

Introduce a Quotation with the Word *That* One of the easiest ways to quote a complete sentence from a source is to use a dependent clause beginning with *that*. As in the following examples, you begin with a tag and a verb and then connect the quoted sentence with *that*.

> Desmond Morris shows that "we evolved as tribal animals, living in comparatively small groups, probably of less than a hundred and we existed like that for millions of years" (66).
>
> Michael Foucault points out that "for a long time, one of the characteristic privileges of sovereign power was the right to decide life and death" (135).

You can also add information to the beginning of a sentence before you introduce the quotation with *that,* as in this example:

> In discussing public speaking, George Plimpton notes that "once the mood of an audience is set, it is difficult to change it, which is why introductions are important" (2).

Here the phrase before Plimpton's name provides a context for the quotation that follows. The quotation itself does not refer to public speaking and could in fact refer to writing, but the writer's opening phrase clarifies Plimpton's topic.

Use Block Quotations Sometimes you might want to quote more than a sentence or two. You use a **block quotation** for such long quotations. How long is long? Some style manuals say fifty words. Others recommend one hundred. Use fifty as a general rule unless your instructor specifies otherwise.

When you introduce a block quotation in a finished paper, drop down one extra space (a total of three spaces in a double-spaced paper). Then indent the quotation ten spaces from the left margin if you are typing and roughly one inch if you are writing by hand. If the quotation is the beginning of a paragraph, indent the first line three more spaces to show the paragraph. Do not use quotation marks around the quotation. The block form tells the reader that the information is quoted. The following is an example of a long quotation in a student paper. Notice how the student leads up to the quotation with her own sentence and then follows the quotation with a discussion of her point. Notice also that the quotation is *not* in quotation marks.

Ken Purdy shows that dishonest repairmen will prey on women very often:

An Ellenville, N.Y., woman, Mrs. Marian Talken, had trouble with her clothes dryer. The repairman told her it needed a new drive-shaft and bearings. The bill was $72 and when the original trouble recurred, he wouldn't come back. Another repairman charged $13 to take the dryer apart and show Mrs. Talken that the same old drive-shaft was still in business at the same old spot (14).

Mrs. Talken's experience is unfortunate and is one of many examples of women being victimized by repairmen. But this is happening less because women today are becoming wiser about cars and appliances as their interests broaden with their independence.

Block quotations enable you to include a fairly long piece of the source. You can often use them to support your thesis. Or, as this student did, you can use them to set up a point of disagreement. When you use a block quotation, make sure that you follow with some discussion of your own. Don't just put the quotation in and leave the reader to figure out why it is there. Also, use block quotations sparingly. A paper with many of them will look as if you are merely stringing together information from sources without using your own ideas.

Use Ellipsis Points in Quotations   Suppose you want to quote only part of a sentence. If you cut something from the beginning of the sentence, you simply work the quotation into your sentence without losing the meaning of the source. If you cut something in the middle or at the end of a quotation because you don't need the whole quotation, then you use **ellipsis points.** Ellipsis points are spaced periods that tell readers that something has been left out of the quotation. The following example shows how ellipsis points work in practice.

Source
> At a newly established taste and smell clinic at the University of Connecticut at Farmington, researchers are finding that the overwhelming majority of patients complaining of a loss of taste really have something wrong with their ability to smell. The clinic is one of two "chemosensory" research and treatment centers (the other is at the University of Pennsylvania) recently established under grants from the National Institute of Neurological and Communicative Disorders and Stroke, in part to help the more than two million American adults who cannot smell and taste normally.
> Jane E. Brody, "What the Nose Knows," p. 1

Quotation in a Student Paper
> According to Jane E. Brody, at the University of Connecticut there is a taste and smell clinic which "is one of two 'chemosensory' research and treatment centers (the other is at the University of Pennsylvania) recently established . . . in part to help the more than two million American adults who cannot smell and taste normally" (1).

Notice that the ellipsis points in the middle of the sentence were used in place of the information about the clinics' grants. The student chose to cut this information because her purpose in the paragraph was to show how people with taste and smell disorders are being helped. She really did not need to say how the clinics were funded.

Suppose the student's purpose had been to emphasize how medical clinics are funded. Then she might have quoted the information about the grants but cut the information about the people. Compare the following example with the one preceding.

Quotation in a Student Paper

> Recently, funding has been provided to clinics which study rare medical problems. According to Jane E. Brody, the University of Connecticut at Farmington has set up a clinic to study problems with taste and smell. This clinic "is one of two 'chemosensory' research and treatment centers (the other is at the University of Pennsylvania) recently established under grants from the National Institute of Neurological and Communicative Disorders and Stroke ..." (1).

In this example the writer emphasizes funding, not the benefits of the clinic for people. The purpose of her paper was to show how funding supports medical clinics.

Use Square Brackets in Quotations   Sometimes a quotation will not make sense in your sentence unless you change a word to fit the context of your paper or the grammar of the sentence. Suppose you write:

> Ken Purdy says that "now it seems to me that it hasn't been done at all" (10).

Seems to *you* or to Purdy? What hasn't been done? The pronoun *it* has no noun to refer to. Notice how the words in **square brackets** clear up these questions:

> Ken Purdy says that "now it seems to [him] that [repair work] hasn't been done at all" (10).

Although brackets can be handy in integrating quotations, avoid using them too much. Instead, try to choose quotations that can be worked in without brackets, or paraphrase the source. Reserve brackets for important quotations that won't fit any other way.

Writing from Sources: The Mechanics

■ Documenting Your Sources

If you paraphrase, summarize, and quote your sources correctly, you are on your way to writing a successful researched essay and avoiding plagiarism. But to complete the job, you need to document your sources. This means giving credit to the writers whose ideas and words you have integrated into your essay.

When you use a source's ideas or words in your essay, you need to show the reader who and where they come from. If you include a tag, the reader will know whose ideas they are. You also need to use parenthetical citation, that is, to give the page number of the source where those ideas are found.

■ Preparing a List of Works Cited

When you write researched essays, you usually include a list of the sources at the end of the paper with all the information about each source: author, title, date and place of publication, publisher, and so on. If readers want to read more of a source, they can find it and look up the pages cited in parentheses in your paper.

This list of sources is called a **list of works cited.** You begin it on a new page of your paper, and at the top of it you write "Works Cited." For short papers in college, you may not be required to include this list if your instructor is familiar with the source or sources, as in the case of a paper written in response to a textbook chapter or some newspaper articles. For longer essays and term papers, you almost always need to include a list of works cited.

Each type of source has a particular form that you must use when putting it on the list. The following examples conform to the style of the Modern Language Association, an organization of English teachers. This style is widely used in many fields, but as you advance in your major, you should find out whether your field has its own style. For most college writing this style is acceptable.

Once a source is on the list in the proper form, it is called an **entry.** As you take more advanced writing courses, you will learn about the proper style for citing many different kinds of sources. This section presents a few of the more common ones.

A Book with One Author

A book with one author is the simplest of entries, and the same style is used no matter what kind of book you are entering, as long as it has only one author.

Gray, Michael. *Song and Dance Man: The Art of Bob Dylan.* New
    York: Dutton, 1974.

1. The author's name is written last name first, followed by a comma, first name, and a period.
2. Second is the title of the book, followed by a period. Titles of books are printed in italics, but when you type or handwrite them, underline them.
3. Third is the city where the book was published, followed by a colon. (You do not need to add the state for books published in the United States.)
4. Next is the name of the publisher, in shortened form.
5. Last is the date the book was published, followed by a period.

    The information about the city, the publisher, and the date is printed on the title page or copyright page of most books.
    Notice that the first line of the entry is placed against the margin. Any line after the first is indented five spaces.

A Book with More Than One Author

When a book has two authors, use this form for your entry:

Kinnear, Thomas C., and Kenneth L. Bernhardt. *Principles of
    Marketing.* Glenview: Scott, 1986.

1. The first author's name is written with last name first, a comma, and first name, just as in an entry for a book with one

author. The first author's name is the one that appears first on the title page of the book. (The names are not necessarily in alphabetical order.)
2. Write *and,* the name of the second author in regular order, first name is first, last name last. Then put a period.
3. The rest of the information follows the same form used for a book with one author. Notice that *Scott* is the shortened form for the publisher Scott, Foresman.

For a book with more than two authors, use this form:

Divine, Robert A., et al. *America: Past and Present.* Glenview: Scott, 1986.

1. The first author's name is in the same form as in the other entries for books, but it is followed by a comma, the words "et al.," and a period. (*Et al.* means "and others" in Latin.)
2. The remaining information is in the same order as the information for books with one or two authors.

An Essay in a Book

Sometimes essays appear in books by other authors or in collections of essays put together by an editor. When you use such a source, write its entry this way:

Curtin, Sharon. "Aging in the Land of the Young." *Patterns of Exposition 8.* Ed. Randall E. Decker. Boston: Little, 1982. 255–58.

1. The name of the author of the essay follows the same pattern as in other entries: last name, comma, first name, period.
2. Next comes the title of the essay, followed by a period and placed in quotation marks.
3. After the underlined title of the book and a period comes *Ed.,*

the abbreviation for *editor,* and then the editor's name, in regular order.
4. The city, publisher, and year of publication follow, and then the page numbers on which the essay appears, followed by a period.

Sources in Magazines

Often you may use an article, essay, or column from a magazine. Entries for sources from magazines have different styles depending on whether the magazine is published each week or each month. For a source in a weekly magazine, use this form:

Zucker, Seymour. "The Good News Behind the Upturn in Interest Rates." *Business Week* 12 Mar. 1984: 83.

1. The author's name is written with last name first, a comma, first name, and a period.
2. The title of the article is followed by a period and is placed in quotation marks.
3. Next is the title of the magazine. Underline it, but do not put a period after it.
4. Next is the day of the month the magazine was published, followed by the month and year and a colon. There are no commas or periods between title, day, month, and year. All the months *except* May, June, and July are abbreviated to three or four letters.
5. Last is the page number on which the source appeared.

For a monthly magazine, use this form:

Crenshaw, Ben. "Make More Short Putts." *Golf* Sept. 1982: 58–61.

This is the same form as for a weekly magazine, except that the day of the month is not given.

Sources in Newspapers

Whether you are citing an editorial, an article, a feature, or a column, use the following form for a source from a newspaper:

O'Brien, Dennis. "It's Simply Classical Economics." *USA Today* 3 March 1987: sec. A: 4.

1. All the information up to the abbreviation *sec.* (which stands for *section*) is in the same form as in an entry for a source in a weekly magazine.
2. Following the abbreviation, the "A" indicates that O'Brien's column appeared in section A of the paper, and the colon separates the section letter from the page number. Some papers use letters for sections, others use numbers, and some do not mark sections at all. If sections are not marked, just put the page number after the colon following the date.

Interviews

Sometimes interviews are printed in magazines, and sometimes you might interview someone yourself and then use the information in your paper, either paraphrased or quoted. In your paper, you do not use parenthetical references to an interview you conducted verbally, although you do use a tag and you place the interview in the list of works cited. There are two kinds of interview entries: one for a personal interview and another for a telephone interview.

Volkers, Judy. Personal interview. 21 June 1987.
Brackney, James, Police Commissioner. Telephone interview. 14 March 1988.

1. The name of the person comes first, with last name first, a comma, and a period.
2. If the person's title is important, put that next, followed by a period, before indicating the type of interview.
3. Next indicate the type of interview.

4. Last is the date in this order: day, month, and year without commas between them and with a period at the end.

These are sample entries for common sources. There are, however, different forms for other kinds of sources, such as scholarly journals, books in volumes, government reports, and so on. If you use a source and you do not know how to make an entry for it, you can find the proper style in *MLA Handbook for Writers of Research Papers,* 3rd ed. (New York: MLA, 1988), or you can look in a grammar book or ask your instructor.

CHAPTER 4

Writing the Single-Source Essay

As you begin to write researched essays, the methods you learned in Chapter 3 — paraphrasing, summarizing, using quotations — will help you convey the ideas in the source. However, after beginning writers have learned to paraphrase and summarize, they sometimes think that a source essay should merely retell what the source says, without including what they themselves want to say on the topic. Just the opposite is true. Along with what the source says, your opinions, observations, questions, and ideas will make up the content of your essay. If readers just wanted to know what a source says, they could simply read it instead of your essay. What you have to say is the most important part of your essay.

This chapter concentrates on writing in response to one source. This type of writing is common in daily communication as well as in college assignments. A plant manager might be asked to write in response to a government inspection that found unsafe conditions in the plant. A sales manager might write an explanation responding to a report showing decreasing sales in his or her department.

In college, the single-source researched essay is equally common. An elementary education major might be asked to give her opinion of some educator's theory of teaching. An engineering major might write an essay arguing against a professional essay that says that plastic pipe works better than copper for certain types of plumbing. Or any student might be asked to write an essay giving an opinion of an idea stated in a textbook.

The process you learned for writing essays from personal experience and observation also works when you are writing in response to a source. You will use invention strategies to discover ideas about the source. You will have to read and reread your draft as you write. And you will revise and edit the essay before it is finished. Because you are integrating the ideas from the source with your own ideas, the content of the essay will differ from the content of a personal essay, and, therefore, the product will be different. The process, however, is very similar, except that the reading of the source will become part of the process. To write about a source you must know what it says and for what purpose the writer has written.

Finding the Purpose of the Source

Chapter 2 discussed various strategies for reading. As you read a source you are going to respond to in an essay, you will need to put these strategies to work: annotating, finding main ideas, building a context, and so on. Also, you will need to apply some of what you know about writing. For example, you know that writers have a purpose in mind as they write. As you read, look for the writer's purpose, because knowing it will help you find your own purpose when you respond to the source.

The purpose for writing can vary. A writer may merely want to inform his or her audience by presenting information without opinions. Or the writer may want to persuade the audience or argue a point, giving his or her opinions about the information. Compare the following paragraphs.

> Drowning is the second leading cause of accidental death for people between the ages of 4 and 44, according to the American National Red Cross. Twenty-eight percent of those drowned are children under 15 years old. Seven out of ten of them are boys.
>
> Carla Stephens, "Drownproofing"

> For 30 years now, this nation has been on a relentless expensive high-technology binge, forging for itself the machines and systems that are supposed to underpin — and to presage —

our 21st-century lives. The only trouble is that all this high technology not only doesn't seem to be solving our problems, it actually looks to be compounding them.

Kirkpatrick Sale, "The 'Miracle' of Technofix"

Both paragraphs come from the beginning of essays, and you can already guess the purpose of each essay. Stephen's statistics on drowning inform her audience of the danger it poses. In her essay she goes on to present methods for teaching children how to avoid dangerous situations when swimming. While she certainly wants the audience to realize the importance of teaching children water safety, she achieves her purpose by informing with facts. Sale, in contrast, begins with an attack on technology. His claim that it causes more problems than it solves is obviously an opinion because many people believe the opposite. Following this opinion, he presents a series of examples to try to persuade the reader to accept his argument against technology. As the essay continues, Sale argues that solutions to the world's problems must come from people, not technology.

If you are writing an essay arguing that some form of technology is more trouble than it is worth, you might be able to draw on Sale's essay for support. Suppose your essay argues that the possible dangers of nuclear power plants outweigh the value of the energy they produce. Though Sale covers technology in general, you might be able to use some of his opinions because your essay would have a similar purpose — to persuade people to question a form of technology. In contrast, if you are writing in favor of some form of technology — say, the use of computers in schools — you could show how Sale overlooks some of the benefits technology provides. But whatever your topic, recognizing Sale's purpose would help you come up with your own.

■ Invention and the Single-Source Essay

As you are discovering the purpose of a source, whether it is a magazine article or a textbook chapter, ideas come to your mind. If you are reading an article in *Time* magazine about a new trade agreement between the United States and Japan, you might wonder how the agreement will affect automobile prices. You also might question whether the agreement will create or eliminate jobs. In short, you will be thinking and trying to make your own sense of the article, for as you saw in Chapter 2, reading is an active process. Though you would not annotate an article you read just for information or pleasure, if you are reading something to write about it, annotation will help you to discover ideas. As a result, your annotations will be part of the invention stage as they become items on a brainstorming list, spokes on a cluster diagram, ideas for freewriting, or answers to the journalist's questions. In other words, annotation is the beginning of invention when you write in response to a source.

Read the following short essay, noting the student annotations and the brainstorming list that follows.

FROM *The Great Chain of Life*
Joseph Wood Krutch

Joseph Wood Krutch was born in 1893 and died in 1970. Throughout his life, he thought and wrote on a wide range of topics, from literature to politics to ecology. He worked as a newspaper columnist, professor, and naturalist. This essay is a small part of *The Great Chain of Life,* one of the many books Krutch wrote.

It wouldn't be quite true to say that "some of my best friends are hunters." Still, I do number among my respected acquaintances some who not only kill for the sake of killing but count it among their keenest pleasures. And I can think of no better illustration of the fact that men may be separated at some point by a fathomless abyss yet share elsewhere much common ground. To me, it is inconceivable that anyone can think an animal more interesting dead than alive. I can also easily prove, to my own satisfaction, that killing "for sport" is the perfect type of pure evil for which metaphysicians have sometimes sought.

killing for sport = "pure evil"

Most wicked deeds are done because the doer proposes some good for himself. The liar lies to gain some end; the swindler and the thief want things which, if honestly got, might be good in themselves. Even the murderer is usually removing some impediment to normal desires. Though all of these are selfish or unscrupulous, their deeds are not gratuitously evil. But the killer for sport seems to have no such excusable motive. He seems to prefer death to life, darkness to light. He seems to get nothing

sport killer has no reason

Writing the Single-Source Essay 91

power trip

other than the satisfaction of saying: "Something which wanted to live is dead. Because I can bring terror and agony, I assure myself that I have power. Because of me there is that much less vitality, consciousness and perhaps joy in the universe. I am the spirit that denies." When a man wantonly destroys one of the works of man, we call him "Vandal." When he wantonly destroys one of the works of God, we call him "Sportsman."

No.

The <u>hunter-for-food may be as wicked and as misguided as vegetarians say,</u> but he does not kill for the sake of killing. The ranchers and farmers who exterminate all living things not immediately profitable to them may be working against their own best interests; but whether they are or not, they hope to achieve some supposed good by the exterminations. If to do evil, not in the hope of gain but for evil's sake, involves the deepest guilt by which man can be stained, then killing for killing's sake is a

sport killing shows "Reality of evil"

terrifying phenomenon and <u>as strong a proof as we could have of that "<u>reality of evil</u>"</u> with which present-day theologians are concerned.

Brainstorming List

When you make a brainstorming list from your own reading, start with your annotations but also include other points that come to mind. The annotations should be part of the list, but they should generate additional points and ideas. The following is a brainstorming list you might have written in response to Krutch's essay.

Sport hunting true evil to Krutch.
No reason to kill for sport.
What about hunting for food?
Food hunters have reason but still might be wicked.
Killing for sport shows "reality of evil."
Killing for food not as bad.
I agree killing for sport is a kind of power trip.
Sometimes hunting helps animals, like necessary thinning of deer
    herds so the herd won't starve.

What about hunting for profit?
Much depends on whether animals are endangered species.
Almost instinct to hunt.
Kids kill bugs and small animals before they learn better.

Like any brainstorming list, this one needs to be sorted out. One way to begin sorting it is to make two lists: one of the points you might agree with and another of points you might disagree with and points the source overlooks.

Possible Agreement	*Possible Opposition*
No reason to kill for sport.	What about hunting for food?
Sport hunting true evil to Krutch.	Food hunters have reason but still might be wrong.
Killing for sport shows "reality of evil."	Killing for food not as bad.
Killing for sport is a kind of power trip.	Sometimes hunting helps animals, like necessary thinning of deer herds so the herd won't starve.
	What about hunting for money? Much depends on whether animals are endangered species.
	Almost instinct to hunt.
	Kids kill bugs and small animals before they learn better.

A glance at the lists shows that you have more points in opposition to Krutch than in agreement with him. You agree that killing animals for pure sport is wrong. However, the second list raises questions about additional points such as hunting for profit, hunting as a necessary thinning of herds, hunting endangered species, and hunting as possibly an instinct. In comparing these lists, you can begin to discover a purpose: to show that Krutch is partly right about hunting but that in overlooking some aspects of it, he has not seen the reasons for hunting for food. From this purpose, you can then formulate a thesis: Hunting purely for sport is wrong, but in most cases there is nothing wrong with hunting for food and profit.

Writing the Single-Source Essay   93

■ Finding a Purpose and Thesis in Responding to a Source

If you have written even a simple book report in elementary or high school, you have some sense of how the writer's purpose controls what he or she says about the source. In a book report, often your purpose was merely to show your teacher that you read and understood the book. You included a summary of the book's plot or main points, a brief explanation of what they meant, and an evaluation of whether the book was worth reading. The last part of the purpose also generated a thesis on the value of the book.

Likewise, in the examples mentioned at the beginning of this chapter, each writer has a purpose. The plant manager must explain why government inspectors found unsafe conditions and show how those conditions can be corrected. This purpose would lead to a thesis stating agreement with the findings of the inspectors but arguing that the unsafe conditions will be corrected. The elementary education major would attempt to show her audience whether the educator's theory would work if put into practice in a classroom. Her thesis would answer that question.

In college assignments, the professor often will give you a writing assignment along with assigned reading. Thus, you can begin to think about your purpose for writing as you read. Suppose that in a communications course, the professor assigned Don Lago's "Symbols of Mankind" along with this topic:

> Write an essay showing how humans have communicated and still communicate using symbols other than letters and words. Refer to Lago's examples but also show examples that you see in your daily life.

Given such a specific topic, you would know what the purpose of your paper would be even before you wrote it: to show that people still communicate with symbols other than letters and words. And you would have a built-in thesis: People still use symbols other than letters and words to communicate. Your task would be to find examples of such symbols and show how they are similar to those of the primitive people mentioned in Lago's essay.

Sometimes an assignment may not be specific. Suppose you are taking an ecology course and the professor assigns you to read Krutch's essay and write a response to it. Whether you use a brainstorming list, clustering, freewriting, or the journalist's questions, you will have to go through the process of invention to find your purpose and thesis just as we did in the text following Krutch's essay.

■ Organizing and Drafting a Source Essay

If you have defined your purpose and stated a thesis, you are ready to begin organizing and drafting your essay. But remember that just as when you write from personal experience, your thesis and purpose can change as you are writing because your ideas can change while writing.

Beginning with a possible thesis (remember that it can change), you can look back over your brainstorming list (or other invention list) to pick out points to support your thesis. For example, consider the thesis for the essay in response to Krutch's essay:

> Hunting purely for sport is wrong, but in most cases there is nothing wrong with hunting for food and profit.

Since the first part of the thesis agrees with Krutch, you can evaluate the list of points under possible agreement. Suppose that in evaluating these, you find that although you are against sport hunting, you do not consider it the "pure evil" Krutch does. You do, however, agree that there is no reason to kill for sport, so you decide that this point will be the topic of your first body paragraph (don't worry about the introduction; you can write it later, even last). You also notice that the only reason Krutch sees for killing for sport is that the hunter feels a kind of power. With these two points in mind, you can brainstorm again:

Only reason for sport killing is feeling of power.
Hunter doesn't use animal for food.
Hunter hangs up heads or skins, trophies.
Brags to his friends.
Not too brave to shoot an animal with a powerful gun.
Hunter feels brave, though.

Once you have some notes for your first body paragraph, you can then decide what you will say in the following paragraphs and in what order you will arrange your ideas. To do so, you can examine the list of points to support the second part of your thesis: that there is nothing wrong with hunting for food and profit. As you look through the list, you can discard points that you cannot use to support the thesis: children killing insects, the possibility that hunting is an instinct (this would be impossible to support in a short essay). You are left with three issues to develop to oppose Krutch's argument and support your own: hunting for food, hunting for profit, hunting as a means of thinning deer herds.

At this point, you can decide on the order in which you will cover these points. For instance, after your first body paragraph agreeing with Krutch's criticism of sport hunting, you might arrange the paragraphs in which you disagree in this order:

Paragraph defending hunting for food.
Paragraph on how hunting can thin deer herds to reduce starvation among deer.
Paragraph on hunting for profit.

As you draft the essay, you might find that you need more than one paragraph to cover one of the points, or you might decide to change the order of the paragraphs. You could do either one while drafting the essay or later in revising it. However, if you are not quite sure what you want to say on each point, you should do some brainstorming before drafting. You might make a brainstorming list like the following.

Hunting for Food
Not endangered species, plentiful animals.
Meat in supermarkets comes from animals killed for food too, no difference.
Laws against how many animals you can kill, even for food.
One deer provides lots of meals.
Good to freeze deer meat.
People in rural areas hunt a lot.

Once you have this much information for each paragraph, either in your head or on a list, you are ready to begin drafting the essay. In drafting, you need to organize and develop each paragraph as much as possible.

■ Organizing and Developing Body Paragraphs

The paragraphs in an essay responding to a source should focus on and develop a point that supports your thesis. As you gain experience in responding to sources, you will discover your own means of organization. The following sections discuss several ways to organize body paragraphs so that they draw on the source while allowing you to develop your ideas.

The Three-Step Method

The **three-step method** of organizing a paragraph works like a conversation. First, you state one point from the source. Second, you state your opinion of that point. Third, you back up your opinion with examples. This method can take different forms. You can use one form when you agree with an idea in the source, another when you disagree, another when you have mixed feelings about the idea, and still another when you want to raise an issue not mentioned in the source.

Agreeing with the Source To use the three-step method to agree, pose these three questions:

1. What is the idea from the source and who said it? (Start with a tag and then paraphrase, quote, or use a combination of paraphrase and quotation.)
2. Why do you agree with the source?
3. What are your agreements or examples to support your agreement?

As you answer the questions, you will generate the information you need to develop a body paragraph, as the following example shows.

Step 1: Krutch says that killing animals just for sport is "pure evil."
Step 2: I agree because, as Krutch says, there is no reason to kill for sport except to gain a feeling of power.
Step 3: For example, take a big-game hunter who displays the

heads of the animals on the wall of a den. This is just a way for the hunter to show off to others that he is brave. But really he is not because even a lion is no match for a high-powered rifle. And since people do not eat lions, all the hunter gets is the skin and the head, which are just trophies to show off.

As you can see, step 3 requires that you develop examples to support the agreement with Krutch stated in step 2. At this point, it may be necessary to return to the brainstorming list to come up with ideas and examples. At other times, you may have the topic more clearly in mind, and you can develop step 3 just by writing down your response to the question. Whatever the case, if step 3 is not fully developed, the paragraph will not be very specific. But if you think carefully about all three steps, you will end up with a well-developed body paragraph. Consider the paragraph based on the preceding example:

> Krutch says that killing animals just for sport is "pure evil." I agree because, as Krutch says, there is no reason to kill for sport except to gain a feeling of power. For example, a big-game hunter who displays the heads of the animals on the wall of a den is just showing off to others that he is brave. But really he is not very brave because even a lion is no match for a high-powered rifle. And since people do not eat lions, all the hunter gets is the skin and the head, which are just trophies to feed his ego.

Disagreeing with the Source Just as you can use the three-step method to agree with a point in the source, you can also use it to disagree. For instance, the second part of the thesis in response to Krutch's essay says that most of the time it is acceptable to hunt for food. Krutch does not consider the "hunter-for-food" as evil as the sport hunter but says he may be "wicked and ... misguided." The response essay disagrees. To use the three-step method for disagreeing, pose these questions:

1. What is the idea from the source and who said it? (Start with a tag and then paraphrase, quote, or use a combination of paraphrase and quotation.)
2. Why do you disagree with the source?

3. What are your arguments or examples to support your disagreement?

Again, you answer the questions to develop the paragraph. Here is a sample paragraph with each step marked:

> (Step 1) Krutch claims that people who hunt for food "may be as wicked and misguided as the vegetarians sometimes say" (35). (Step 2) Krutch overlooks the fact that many people in rural areas hunt to help feed their families. (Step 3) Butchered and frozen, a deer can provide many meals for a family, and eating the meat from an animal killed by a hunter is no different from eating supermarket meat. In both cases, the animal was killed for food. Game laws prevent senseless killing, but even if they did not exist, hunters should not kill more food than they or their families can eat. Also, they should never hunt endangered species, but there is nothing wrong with hunting to feed a family.

Writing a Mixed Response   Sometimes you will find two closely related points in a source. You may agree with one but disagree with the other, yet because the points are closely related, you want to respond to them in the same paragraph. You can use the three-step method in two different ways when you have such mixed feelings.

To stress agreement, use these questions:

1. What are the conflicting points from the source? (Start with a tag and then paraphrase, quote, or use a combination of paraphrase and quotation to state both points.)
2. What point do you disagree with and why? Give examples.
3. What point do you agree with and why? Begin with a transition to show contrast (such as *but, however, on the other hand, nevertheless*) and then state the point you agree with and give reasons.

As you read the following sample paragraph with the steps marked, notice how step 2, unlike in the earlier forms, is further developed. That is, to stress your agreement with part of the idea, you have to first show the part you disagree with.

> (Step 1) Krutch compares sport hunters to murderers, saying that the murderers' "deeds are not gratuitously evil" (35). (Step 2) With this comparison, Krutch is too extreme. Even though a murderer may have a motive, killing a person is worse than killing an animal because people, unlike animals, have hopes, dreams, and emotions that animals do not feel. (Step 3) Nevertheless, Krutch is right to show sport hunting as "gratuitously evil." The word "gratuitous" means "for no reason," and to kill without reason, even an animal, makes no sense. It is, as Krutch says, "killing for killing's sake" (35).

To stress disagreement, you merely reverse the order of steps 2 and 3. In other words, your paragraph puts material showing agreement in the middle and then ends on a note of disagreement.

> (Step 1) Krutch compares sport hunters to murderers, saying that the murderers' "deeds are not gratuitously evil." (Step 2) Krutch is right to show sport hunting as "gratuitously evil." The word "gratuitous" means "for no reason," and to kill without reason, even an animal, makes no sense. It is, as Krutch says, "killing for killing's sake" (35). (Step 3) Nevertheless, with this comparison, Krutch is too extreme. Even though a murderer may have a motive, killing a person is worse than killing an animal because people, unlike animals, have hopes, dreams, and emotions that animals do not feel.

Now the disagreement is stressed because it comes last in the paragraph. When do you stress agreement? When do you stress disagreement? That depends on your thesis. The end of the paragraph serves as a "last word" on the point the whole paragraph develops. Thus, it should follow from the thesis of your whole essay. If you are using the thesis presented earlier in response to Krutch's essay, you will stress disagreement because that thesis generally disagrees with Krutch. The end of the paragraph should always agree with your position in your thesis. Otherwise, you will sound as if you are changing your opinion halfway through the essay, and your audience will become confused.

Raising a Point Not Mentioned in the Source Sometimes you may read a source and find that the source does not cover some important points about the topic. The brainstorming list in response to Krutch contains a point about hunting for profit, something Krutch never talks about. You can, however, discuss the point, using the following questions.

1. What is the point that the source does not mention?
2. Why is this point important?
3. What examples support the importance of this point?

You might write the following paragraph after answering those questions.

(Step 1) Krutch fails to mention that sometimes hunting can be a source of income for people in need. (Step 2) If the animals being hunted are not endangered species, a person should be allowed to earn a supplemental income by hunting. (Step 3) A friend of mine, Kurt Olson, traps raccoon and fox each winter and sells the pelts. Both animals are plentiful, and both are nuisances to farmers and rural residents because they prey on chickens and pets. So while Kurt is helping rid the area of pests, he is also earning money that he uses to help pay his college tuition. During the winter, other trappers in the area depend on the money they earn to help support their families.

The Three-Step Method Turned Upside Down

Sometimes you can put the idea from a source last in a paragraph, in a sense turning the **three-step method upside down.** This method works best when you agree with the source, but it also can work when you disagree or raise a point the source does not mention. It won't work, however, for handling mixed feelings about a point. Examine each of the following paragraphs and compare it with the related example of the three-step method.

Agreement

(Step 1, your point) There is no reason to kill for sport except to gain a feeling of power. (Step 2, support for your point) For example, a big-game hunter who displays the heads

Writing the Single-Source Essay   101

of the animals on the wall of a den is just showing off to others that he is brave. But really he is not very brave because even a lion is no match for a high-powered rifle. And since people do not eat lions, all the hunter gets is the skin and the head, which are just trophies to feed his ego. (Step 3, support for your point from the source) As Krutch says, killing animals just for the sport of it is "pure evil" (35).

Disagreement

(Step 1, your point) Many people in rural areas hunt to help feed their families. (Step 2, support for your point) Butchered and frozen, a deer can provide many meals for a family, and eating the meat from an animal killed by a hunter is no different from eating supermarket meat. In both cases, the animal was killed for food. Game laws prevent senseless killing, but even if they did not exist, hunters should not kill more food than they or their families can eat. Although hunters should never kill endangered species, even for food, there is nothing wrong with hunting to feed a family. (Step 3, your disagreement with Krutch) So Krutch is wrong to claim that people who hunt for food "may be as wicked and misguided as the vegetarians sometimes say" (35).

Issue Not Mentioned in Source

(Step 1, your point) If the animals being hunted are not endangered species, a person should be allowed to earn a supplemental income by hunting. (Step 2, support for your point) A friend of mine, Kurt Olson, traps raccoon and fox each winter and sells the pelts. Both animals are plentiful, and both are nuisances to farmers and rural residents because they prey on chickens and pets. So while Kurt is helping rid the area of pests, he is also earning money that he uses to help pay his college tuition. During the winter, other trappers in the area depend on the money they earn to help support their families. (Step 3, pointing out that Krutch ignores the issue) In criticizing hunting, Krutch doesn't mention that sometimes hunting can be a source of income for people in need.

Whether you use the regular three-step method or turn it upside down often depends on how you perceive the issue as you are drafting. Sometimes you may have the issue clearly focused, so you start with the source. And sometimes you may write your way into an idea and then find a point in the source that backs you up or that your paragraph shows to be in error.

Paragraphs Without Reference to the Source

Sometimes, even though the whole of your essay is responding to a source, you may write paragraphs that develop only your ideas. There is nothing wrong with such paragraphs as long as the whole of the essay deals with and mentions the source at some points. Paragraphs with only your ideas may come before or after paragraphs that deal directly with the source. The first of the following two paragraphs is the one disagreeing with Krutch's claims about the "hunter-for-food." The paragraph following it expands on the disagreement but without reference to Krutch.

> Krutch claims that people who hunt for food "may be as wicked and misguided as the vegetarians sometimes say" (35). Krutch overlooks the fact that many people in rural areas hunt to help feed their families. Butchered and frozen, a deer can provide many meals for a family, and eating the meat from an animal killed by a hunter is no different from eating supermarket meat. In both cases, the animal was killed for food. Game laws prevent senseless killing, but even if they did not exist, hunters should not kill more food than they or their families can eat. Also, they should never hunt endangered species, but there is nothing wrong with hunting to feed a family.
>
> Most people who hunt for food hunt legally, killing only their limit of plentiful species. Along with supplying themselves with food, these hunters prevent animals from starving to death. For instance, many deer would starve to death each winter because deer herds need more food than nature provides in a snow-covered forest. In this sense, nature is crueler than hunters.

The second paragraph does not refer to Krutch, yet it adds support for the argument against Krutch's claim that hunting for food may be wicked.

■ Writing an Introduction to a Single-Source Essay

In Chapter 1, you learned various strategies for writing an introduction: raising a question, leading in with examples, quoting a famous person, referring to something you have read, and many others. You also learned that whether you write your introduction first or last does not matter, as long as it accomplishes the following:

1. Getting the reader's attention
2. Introducing the topic
3. Limiting the topic
4. Stating your thesis about the topic

An introduction to a source essay, like any other introduction, should achieve these goals. However, it should also make clear that you are writing in response to a source. There are two common ways to write an introduction to an essay in response to a source.

Opening Summary and Thesis

One introductory strategy presented in Chapter 1 was the reference to something you read. In writing from personal experience and observation, you use that reference as a "jumping-off point."

In writing in response to a source, you refer to what you have read — the source — and then develop the essay in response. This reference to the source, instead of just serving as a way to approach a topic, should briefly summarize the source so that the reader knows what your thesis is responding to. You might write the following introduction to an essay on Krutch's work.

In *The Great Chain of Life,* Joseph Wood Krutch argues that hunters who kill animals just for sport are doing the worst kind of evil. Krutch says that they are worse than liars, thieves, and even murderers because their actions have no purpose other than to make them feel powerful. As for people who hunt for food, Krutch believes they at least have a purpose, but he also says they may be evil too. Hunting purely for sport is certainly wrong, but in most cases there is nothing wrong with hunting for food and profit.

This introduction presents a summary of Krutch's essay, starting with reference to the book it is from and a tag using Krutch's full name the first time it is mentioned. Then with short tags, the paragraph states how Krutch feels about people who hunt for sport and what he implies about those who hunt for food. The thesis of the response essay follows. Thus, the introduction clearly shows what source the essay will respond to, what the source has said on the topic, and what the essay will say in response.

Adding an Introductory Strategy to the Summary and Thesis

Any of the strategies for writing an introduction (discussed in Chapter 1) can be added to the summary and thesis to help get the reader's attention. The following discussion shows how some of them can work with the summary and thesis. Start with the introductory strategy, follow with the brief summary, and then state your thesis. You need to make a smooth transition from the introductory strategy to the summary; pay close attention to how the sample paragraphs move from the introduction to the first mention of Krutch's essay.

Selecting This strategy starts with a straightforward statement about the broad subject area of which the topic is a part, gives brief but specific examples within that subject area, and then focuses on one example for the topic of the essay.

> Sports can be violent. To some people, boxing should be outlawed because the boxer's purpose is to injure his opponent. Other people wonder how something as dangerous as autoracing can be a sport. And others question even the violence of football. To Joseph Wood Krutch, the worse sport is

Writing the Single-Source Essay 105

hunting. In *The Great Chain of Life,* Krutch argues that hunters who kill animals just for sport are doing the worst kind of evil. Krutch says that they are worse than liars, thieves, and even murderers because their actions have no purpose other than to make them feel powerful. As for people who hunt for food, Krutch believes they at least have a purpose, but he also says they may be evil too. Hunting purely for sport is certainly wrong, but in most cases there is nothing wrong with hunting for food and profit.

This introduction begins with a broad subject area, violent sports, and then narrows the subject down to Krutch's topic on hunting. In other words, the writer selected hunting for sport from other violent sports.

Narrating Setting up a scene with a brief narration can grab the reader's attention before moving to the summary.

A tiger strides warily through the jungle, its muscles stretching its gold and black coat. It senses danger as it moves into a clearing to confront whatever is giving off a scent unlike any other in the jungle. It never finds its adversary, for in a moment it lies dead, streams of red blood mixing with its black and gold stripes. Three men, feeling triumphant, pull up in a jeep, shoot it once more to be sure, and then cart it back to civilization where its head and skin will hang on a wall or cover a floor. In *The Great Chain of Life,* Joseph Wood Krutch argues that hunters who kill animals just for sport are doing the worst kind of evil. Krutch says that they are worse than liars, thieves, and even murderers because their actions have no purpose other than to make them feel powerful. As for people who hunt for food, Krutch believes they at least have a purpose, but he also says they may be evil too. Hunting purely for sport is certainly wrong, but in most cases there is nothing wrong with hunting for food.

The brief scene in the narration gives the reader an idea of the beauty of the tiger and of the uncaring nature of the hunter. Thus it supports Krutch's point about the brutality of hunting for sport. At the same time, this brutality is in contrast to the idea for hunting for food, which the essay will argue is acceptable.

Asking Questions   A question or two can often make the reader curious before you begin the discussion of the source.

>   Is a man who kills his limit during deer season and then butchers and freezes the meat so his family has food the same as a man who shoots a lion on a safari, mounts the head in his office, uses the skin for a throw rug in front of his fireplace, but has no taste or use for the meat? This and other questions about hunting are implied in Joseph Wood Krutch's *The Great Chain of Life*. Krutch argues that hunters who kill animals just for sport are doing the worst kind of evil. He says that they are worse than liars, thieves, and even murderers because their actions have no purpose other than to make them feel powerful. As for people who hunt for food, Krutch believes they at least have a purpose, but he also says they may be evil too. Hunting purely for sport is certainly wrong, but in most cases there is nothing wrong with hunting for food and profit.

Here the question sets up the contrast between the hunter who kills for food and the hunter who kills for sport. After the summary, the thesis then answers the opening question.

Surprising the Reader   Any statement that surprises readers will usually get their attention.

>   Killing an animal can be worse than killing a person. This is one point Joseph Wood Krutch makes in *The Great Chain of Life*. Krutch argues that hunters who kill animals just for sport are doing the worst kind of evil. He says that they are worse than liars, thieves, and even murderers because their actions have no purpose other than to make them feel powerful. As for people who hunt for food, Krutch believes they at least have a purpose, but he also says they may be evil too. Hunting purely for sport is certainly wrong, but in most cases there is nothing wrong with hunting for food and profit.

Writing the Single-Source Essay   107

The opening statement needs much explanation because few people would agree with it; thus, readers would want to find out when killing an animal is worse than killing a person.

Using some kind of introductory strategy along with the summary and thesis can liven up the opening of your essay. There is one catch, though. Sometimes the introductory strategy, when added to the summary, will make the introduction seem rather long. If you feel your introduction is too long, you can cut it into two paragraphs, making the introductory strategy the first paragraph and the summary with thesis the second.

■ Writing a Conclusion to a Single-Source Essay

The conclusion of an essay serves three purposes:

1. To stress the importance of your thesis
2. To leave a lasting impression
3. To give the essay a sense of completeness

Given these purposes, a conclusion should restate the thesis in different words, be more general than the body paragraphs, and be short enough that it does not make the reader forget the body.

The conclusion of a source essay should have these purposes and qualities, but, like the rest of the essay, it should also refer to the source. The following paragraph is a possible conclusion, using the question strategy, for the essay in response to Krutch.

> All hunters are not the same. Krutch is correct in condemning people who shoot animals merely for the thrill of it. And though he admits that people who hunt for food have a purpose, his suspicions that they may be wicked are misguided. The sport hunter is evil; the food hunter is practical. Most people can easily condemn the hunter who shoots an animal to hang its head on a wall, but how easy is it to condemn the hunter who shoots an animal to put food on the table?

The conclusion opens with a very general statement that recalls the thesis. The following reference to Krutch then restates his main arguments before moving to a fairly specific restatement of the thesis, which contrasts evil and practicality. The closing question furthers the contrast but places the responsibility on the reader to make a judgment.

Writing a conclusion to a source essay is no more difficult than writing a conclusion to any other essay. Just comment generally on the source and keep the purposes of conclusions in mind.

■ Revising and Editing Checklists

To help you revise and edit an essay that responds to a source, ask yourself the following questions.

Revising

1. Is the title of the source mentioned in your introduction?
2. Do you use the author's full name the first time you cite it with a tag?
3. Does the introduction briefly summarize the thesis of the source?
4. Does the essay refer to the source at various points so that it avoids drifting off into a personal essay?
5. Are the source's points clearly tagged so that the reader can tell them from your own?
6. Do you present the source's ideas accurately and clearly when you paraphrase them?
7. Do you use your own words and sentence structure when you paraphrase?
8. Do your responses logically follow or lead to the source's ideas? In other words, are you and the source talking about the same issue?
9. If you have used the three-step method, are all steps clear, and is step 3 fully developed?

10. Do your body paragraphs end in agreement with your thesis?
11. Does your conclusion mention the source as it reasserts your thesis?

Editing

1. If the source is a book, have you underlined the title?
2. If the source is an essay, have you placed the title in quotation marks?
3. If you quote the source, have you used its *exact* words in every instance?
4. If you have left words out of a quotation, have you used ellipsis points?
5. In integrating quotations, have you avoided sentence errors such as comma splices and run-on sentences?
6. When you have included ideas from the source, have you cited them in your paper with parenthetical citation (page numbers in parentheses)?
7. If required, at the end of the essay have you included a "works cited" entry for the source? If so, have you used the proper entry form?

CHAPTER 5

Writing the Multiple-Source Essay

Just as you may write in response to one source, you may sometimes compare and contrast two sources or you may draw on several sources. Like most writing, multiple-source writing occurs both on the job or at school. A sales manager, for example, would probably consult many market reports and economic sources before writing a plan for the company's yearly sales campaign. A scientist working on a particular experiment would read what other scientists found in similar experiments and refer to their writings when he wrote a report on the experiment. And any student writing a term paper is writing a multiple-source essay. This chapter will teach you the basics of writing a multiple-source essay so that you can write a term paper, or any other paper requiring sources.

■ Responding to Two Sources

A common type of multiple-source essay asks you to compare and contrast two sources. You have read Joseph Wood Krutch's essay from *The Great Chain of Life,* which generally condemned hunting; now read another opinion on the topic.

In Defense of Hunting
John C. Dunlap

Born in 1946, John C. Dunlap has written articles and essays in sporting magazines such as *Rod and Reel, Field and Stream,* and *Sports Afield.* In addition to writing, he teaches high school in Vermont. This essay first appeared in *Time* magazine.

"What are your moral justifications for hunting?"

The man who asked me this is my neighbor, a well-educated and thoughtful newcomer to our little valley in northeast Vermont. He and his partner have just built a small house across the way. We want to be friends; there are going to be difficulties.

My first reaction is to trot out all the standard, unconvincing arguments about game management, about hunting as a last vestige of our primitive selves. It's easy, after so many years of assault, to feel defensive about this subject. Instead, I have a Socratic inspiration.

"What are your justifications for *not* hunting?" I ask.

So I get to listen to *his* standard unconvincing arguments: the sacredness of life; the obligation not to interfere with its mechanisms; the storm of death; the suffering; the continuing evolution of man.

The hypocrisy of all this is staggering.

Vegetarians

The only opponents I'll listen to for long are vegetarians. I won't listen a minute to meat eaters who pay the butcher and supermarket to kill, package, and distribute their meals. But even the sophistic arguments of the vegetarians inevitably irritate me. It's funny, they think I'm kidding when I ask if plants feel pain. Plants can fill their lives with peace, and their stomachs with nourishment, plant life fashions dazzling displays of color and shape and even responds to classical music. But when the gardner approaches with pruning shears, suddenly plants are numb and indifferent.

I am not a theologian who can argue complicated precepts of morality. I am, I hope, a reasonably intelligent and sensitive man who tries to think clearly about what he does. And what I do is hunt, and sometimes kill.

So who doesn't? Does the power that orchestrates affairs in our universe accord a deer more importance than a fly quivering in a strip of sticky tape? Show me where. No sensible person will argue that significance is related to size — but there are few advocates of the small.

The universe shows no less enthusiasm in exterminating life than in creating it. What do all the opponents of hunting think the sweet-singing "feathered glories" are doing, carving graceful arcs in the evening air? They're killing, just as fast as they can. Even doves, man-made symbols of gentleness, pick through the farmer's silage bins down the road, looking for juicy bugs to snip in half and devour. And the jewel-like trout, darting among the mossy rocks — they're busy killing, too. The foxes and bobcats of our forests are predators as well, and it's fortunate for their prey that they are. As wise Theseus points out at the conclusion of Chaucer's "Knight's Tale," death is forever busy "Converting all things back into the source / From which they were derived, to which they course."

Good Intentions

Urban moralists so often seem to have an image of hunting seasons as bloody free-for-alls. They know virtually nothing about the fish and game departments' endless and difficult assessments of herd size and habitat quality. How many "friends of wildlife" have tramped through the deep snows of early April to count the many thousand deer carcasses strewn through the woods? Not many, I bet. Can this "natural" solution to excessive animal numbers be acceptable to them? We interfere everywhere to keep living things happy and healthy and call it progress — but not here. Just as surely as you can rob a man with a pen, so too can deer be killed with good intentions. If we were to outlaw hunting, millions of beasts would suffer and die each year as they competed for limited feed. In fact, social and economic developments have so altered the habitat that we must now assume increased responsibility to manage wildlife intelligently. Who pays for this management? The hunters pay, with their licenses; the opponents talk.

The intelligence and practicality of game management in the form of hunting seasons were proved to me long ago. Most state departments of fish and game have excellent literature explaining their policies and practices better than I am able to do here. I suggest this as beginning reading material for those who condemn hunting; I have yet to argue this issue with someone who was well informed.

Passions

Then again, it seems clear that opponents of hunting fashion their moral stance not on a cosmic model, as they so often say, but on a merely human one. Indeed, arguments on both sides usually come down to passions, and these interest me most. For just as the urban world has largely been stripped of its wildness and suburbs poisoned and thoroughly paved over, it is possible that, given enough time, our very instincts will suffer the same fate: our mysterious inner forests cut down, our spiritual waters polluted and damned. Paradoxically, hunting — which deals in death — can intensify our understanding of life.

So how *can* I do it? I go hunting because I cannot resist prowling out in the dark mornings and the umber dusks — the cracks, as I have heard them described, between the worlds. I go to have shadowy, sometimes violent encounters with my brother animals. I go to watch a silent, indifferent power fill the woods, and see the woods awed in its presence.

Contrasting the Essays for Invention

Before you can write an essay contrasting the Dunlap and Krutch sources, you should list the main points of each. The lists are like brainstorming lists, but you do not put down anything that comes to mind. Rather, you limit yourself to the points from each essay. It helps to place the lists side by side to sort out each author's points.

Krutch	*Dunlap*
Hunting sets people apart from each other.	Dunlap and neighbor disagree on hunting.
Sport hunting true evil.	Hunting no different from eating meat killed for supermarkets.
No reason to kill for sport.	

Sport hunters as bad as
  murderers.
Sport hunters are on a power
  trip, eliminate vitality in
  universe.
Food hunters have reason but
  still might be wicked.
Killing for sport shows "reality
  of evil."

Plants have lives but are killed
  for food.
Insects killed; does size make a
  difference?
All animals in nature kill to
  survive.
Hunting helps game
  management, and license
  fees pay for it.
Hunting brings us closer to
  inner passions, hunt
  "brother animals."

Once you have these lists, you can break the topic down into a list of issues — arguments that are important to the overall argument of whether people should hunt. Each author will not always deal with each issue, so you need to examine both lists to find all the issues. Also, you can raise and list issues of your own. As you list each issue, give one author's opinion on it, then the other's, and finally your own.

Hunting sets people apart.
Krutch: Can't understand how someone could "think an animal
  more interesting dead than alive."
Dunlap: Asks why people do *not* hunt.
Your opinion: People's ideas about hunting depend on their
  background.

Hunting for sport.
Krutch: Worst kind of evil, no reason, power trip to reduce vitality
  in the universe.
Dunlap: Does not comment.
Your opinion: Maybe not as bad as Krutch says, but definitely
  wrong.

Hunting for food.
Krutch: May be as wicked as vegetarians say.
Dunlap: No different than eating supermarket meat or eating plants
  because plants are killed, too, and all of nature is involved in
  killing for survival.

Your opinion: Nothing wrong with hunting for food as long as animals are not endangered species and hunters do not kill more than can be eaten.

Hunting and game management.
Krutch: Does not comment.
Dunlap: Hunting thins deer herds, which is necessary in winter, and license fees help pay for game management.
Your opinion: Hunting for food does help game management as long as hunters do not kill more animals than they are allowed.

Hunting and our relationship to nature.
Krutch: Sport hunters destroy nature.
Dunlap: Hunters get close to their inner passions in confrontations with "brother animals."
Your opinion: Hunting for food is another way to use nature and must be done responsibly, but we should not enjoy killing animals or think of ourselves as animals.

Hunting for profit.
Krutch: Does not comment.
Dunlap: Does not comment.
Your opinion: Hunting or trapping to sell meat or skins is acceptable if animals are not endangered species.

Once you have a list of issues such as this one, you can begin to find your purpose and a possible thesis.

Finding a Thesis and Organizing Your Draft

Like all essays, the essay in response to two sources should have a clear thesis and pattern of organization. Also, as in previous essays, your thesis and pattern of organization can change if in drafting you discover ideas that you did not have when you began. If so, you may have to revise your thesis and your means of supporting it. If you examine your list of issues and can't come up with a thesis to cover all of them, you might begin writing on the one or two issues you feel reasonably certain about. However, often by examining the list, you can find a thesis and pattern of organization to guide you as you write your draft.

Finding a Possible Thesis   In the single-source essay in response to Krutch, you compared the issues on which you agreed with him and those on which you disagreed. The process of finding a thesis to respond to two sources is similar. You first review your list of issues and opinions to see where you agree (or partly agree) with one source, where you agree (or partly agree) with the other, and where you have raised issues not mentioned in either. Then make another list.

Agreement with Krutch
1. Hunting sets people apart, but background is determining factor in whether a person hunts.
2. There is no reason to hunt for sport.

Agreement with Dunlap
1. Hunting sets people apart, but background is determining factor in whether a person hunts.
2. Hunting for food is acceptable.
3. Hunting for food helps game management.
4. Hunting helps define our relationship to nature, though we should not enjoy the violence, as Dunlap seems to.

Additional Issue
   Earning supplemental income by hunting is acceptable. Dunlap would probably agree; Krutch would probably disagree, or at least partly disagree.

   In examining this list, you can see that you agree with Krutch that there is no reason to hunt for sport. You also can see that you not only agree with some of Dunlap's reasons to hunt for food but have added another reason he does not mention. You can begin to try out a possible thesis:

   There is no reason to hunt merely for sport, but there are many good reasons to justify other kinds of hunting.

   This thesis could give you a start. However, the phrase "many good reasons" might strike some readers as vague. You can briefly specify the reasons:

Writing the Multiple-Source Essay   117

> There is no reason to hunt merely for sport, but other kinds of hunting can help define our relationship to nature, provide food, contribute to game management, and offer a means of supplementing income.

This thesis would work, but it may be a little too specific because it locks you into a pattern of organization that you might not find effective as you write the draft. So you might look for alternatives that are more specific than your first attempt but that allow more flexibility than the second.

> Hunting purely for sport is brutal, but not all hunting is a form of brutality.

This thesis allows you not only to show why you believe there is no good reason to hunt for sport but also to separate other kinds of hunting so that you can argue that they are acceptable.

Of course, refining and focusing the thesis can be done at any point in drafting and revising. If you can start with a focused thesis, fine, but even the first thesis, as vague as it is, would give you a start, although you might have to revise it later.

Organizing Your Draft   As always, you can write sections of your draft in any order you wish and arrange them later. Or you can list the issues in the order you want to discuss them and then follow the list as you draft. Just as in drafting the single-source essay, you probably want to discuss your agreement that sports hunting is brutal in the first body paragraph. That way, your readers will know you are not in favor of all hunting before you try to convince them why certain types are acceptable. You might try a list that follows Dunlap's pattern of organization and then add the issue he does not mention:

Hunting for food
Hunting and game management
Hunting and our relationship to nature
Hunting for profit

The advantage of this list is that in putting the issue on hunting for profit last, you would show that you have taken the topic further than both sources because neither Krutch nor Dunlap mentions the issue. However, if you find that this issue does not lead to your most convincing point, you can put it earlier in the essay. Or you might want it to follow the paragraph on hunting for food since both issues show how people use the game they hunt. Likewise, you might see that game management is a way of defining our relationship to nature and put your coverage of it after the more general discussion of hunting and nature. As a result, you would have the following list:

Hunting for food
Hunting for profit
Hunting and our relationship to nature
Hunting and game management

This order might work well because the last body paragraph now covers one of the strongest arguments for hunting. Also, the movement from hunting for personal gain — food and profit — to hunting and the larger questions of nature has a certain logic to it.

As you consider the order in which you will cover the issues, try out various lists. Not only will the lists provide possible patterns for your draft, but they will stimulate your thinking on the topic, causing you to see connections between one issue and another. If you don't find a possible order in which to discuss the issues, you can write about them one at a time and then think about how you will arrange the sections you have written. This method will also help you think about the relationship of issues to one another. Whether you decide on your order first, last, or somewhere in between, this part of the process requires much thought.

■ **Responding to Three or More Sources**

Some writing you do in college and later will ask you to respond to a number of sources on one topic. In college writing, the term paper is the obvious example. You may also find that papers shorter and less formal than term papers can benefit from the use of sources. You have learned how to write in response to one or two sources. Responding to three or more is not much more difficult. The key is to pay careful attention to invention, as you find the sources' opinions and as you develop your own on the various issues. The following four essays first appeared in *USA Today* in 1987, and each deals with the cost of attending colleges. Read them carefully, taking notes as appropriate. Add annotations of your own if you like.

Colleges Must Cut Costs, Help Students
USA Today Editorial

If you were counting on lower inflation to ease the financial pain of sending your children to college, count again.

We may have conquered inflation during the past six years, but college tuitions still increased twice as fast as the cost of living — faster than new houses, health care, energy, food, and cars.

And although inflation has been less than 2 percent, tuition next fall is expected to be 6 percent to 8 percent higher than last September. It may rise 5 percent the year after.

You don't need a college degree to know something's wrong here.

A new study of college costs by the American Council on Education tries to put the tuition increases in the best light. Tuitions haven't increased much more than inflation since 1970, the report says.

That may sound like good news. But it's not. What really counts is how much higher education costs today, and next year, and the next.

Why is tuition going up faster than other costs? "The simple answer," says the report, "is that nobody knows."

Well, it's time somebody found out.

Every time costs rise, college slips beyond the reach of more middle-class families. It's even worse for poor families. Since 1980, the percentage of students from families with less than $30,000 income has fallen from 68 percent to 37 percent.

Student borrowing is five times higher than it was a decade ago. Up to one-half the students leave college with a degree in one hand and a promissory note in the other. Many owe so much they can't afford low-paying public service jobs such as teaching or social work.

The colleges say they need to catch up on faculty and staff salaries, building programs, and maintenance that fell behind during the double-digit inflation days of the '70s.

But these excuses are wearing thin. Colleges have had plenty of time to catch up.

Administrators also point to increased costs for sophisticated equipment, science facilities, computers, books, and the need to compensate for declining federal aid.

But if they can't control these costs, somebody else will. Congress is already under pressure from parents worried that they won't be able to afford college for their children.

Education Secretary William Bennett argues that cutting federal aid will reduce costs. He's wrong.

Cutting student loan and financial aid programs is one of the worst possible ways to balance the federal budget. While tuition trailed inflation in the 1970s, federal student aid more than tripled. When student aid slowed down, college costs took off.

Government officials and educators must work together to increase educational opportunities, not limit them. That means liberal student loan programs, with strong payback provisions. It means restraining spending on campus.

Everybody doesn't want to go to college. But everybody who wants to deserves the chance.

Colleges Must Not Cut Quality to Curb Costs
Sheldon Hackney

Sheldon Hackney is president of the University of Pennsylvania.

Educational opportunities should be determined by a student's abilities and interests, not financial status. The individual student benefits, but so does the nation if students attend the schools that can challenge them.

At Penn, we admit students on their academic qualifications, then work with them to find the necessary financial support. We hold to that policy despite the rising costs and changes in federal student aid that have left most U.S. colleges in a financial crunch.

Higher education is a complex and expensive enterprise. It's labor intensive, and that labor is highly specialized. Top scholars are expensive to attract and retain, especially in fields such as business, law, medicine, science, and engineering, where we compete for employees with the for-profit sector.

The rapid increase in knowledge also has its costs. Major new disciplines are emerging, and simply keeping up with existing ones increases expenses yearly. Lab equipment is more sophisticated and more expensive now, and computers — Penn, for example, has 10,000 computer work stations — have become an integral part of teaching, research, and administration.

In recent years, colleges have assumed a greater burden in providing student financial aid, augmenting state and federal aid with their own funds. This year, more than 40 percent of Penn's students will receive financial aid, including more than $20 million from university resources.

In addition, universities are as large as small cities and require many of the same support services. Penn is the largest private employer in the Philadelphia region; our public safety force is larger than most of the state's 900 municipal police departments; our annual utility costs are upward of $18 million; and insurance costs have doubled in two years.

In response to mounting costs, universities have implemented cost-saving programs, ranging from purchasing stationery at bulk rate to generating their own electrical energy. They have more intelligently managed their endowment portfolios to provide a more secure economic base and better endowment income, and they have approached fund-raising more creatively.

Penn will spend $30 million in endowment income this year and raise more than $140 million in research funding, and more than $50 million from alumni and friends to augment tuition revenue, which covers less than one-half the cost of the education we provide.

Colleges must continue to hold down costs without sacrificing their educational missions. But federal aid is vital both to assist individuals in reaching their potential and to ensure that society will have an educated citizenry, a future generation of doctors, engineers, teachers, and other college-trained professionals, and the benefit of the kind of basic research that is best done by academic institutions.

Taxpayer Subsidies Help Fuel Tuition Hikes
William J. Bennett

A longtime educator, William Bennett wrote this essay when he was secretary of education in Ronald Reagan's administration.

As colleges and universities begin announcing next year's tuition increases, many parents once again find themselves pained and baffled by the skyrocketing cost of college education.

Many colleges have announced tuition increases for next year ranging from 4 percent to, in one case, 20 percent — even though inflation in 1986 was only 1.8 percent.

In fact, tuition has risen at twice the rate of inflation since 1980. No wonder that some 82 percent of the American people worry that college costs will soon be out of reach of most families.

For a while, the higher education establishment denied that much of a problem existed. Recently, though, they have switched gears. The American Council on Education is now encouraging the higher education community to "intensify its efforts to identify the causes of tuition inflation."

This is welcome. But it would be better still if the American Council on Education also urged the higher education community to act to keep tuition inflation down.

Such action is needed. As things now stand, tuition inflation threatens to cancel out the beneficial effects of federal college aid programs.

Instead of helping families meet the cost of a college education, the $14 billion per year federal subsidy seems to enable college administrators to raise prices ever higher.

While the current structure of federal student aid may not cause tuition inflation, there is little doubt that it helps make it possible — because when colleges raise prices, the taxpayers increase their subsidy to help families make up the differences, then colleges raise tuition again, and so on.

We have proposed reforms that would address this problem.

But the primary responsibility for containing education costs cannot lie with the federal government. It lies with our colleges and universities.

No one doubts that there is a lot of fat in some areas of higher education — just as there has been in some areas of U.S. business.

The pressures of economic competition have forced a lot of businesses to slim down and become more cost-efficient. U.S. higher education needs to look to that example, rather than justifying whopping tuition increases by merely saying, as one university official recently said, that "new knowledge is inherently more expensive."

Americans have always been generous when it comes to providing funds for higher education. So we shall remain. But it's time for our colleges and universities to do better at living up to their end of the bargain.

It's Simply Classical Economics
Dennis O'Brien

Dennis O'Brien is president of the University of Rochester.

The most interesting aspect of Secretary of Education William J. Bennett's crusade for collegiate economy is his touching belief that he knows the proper form of the college curriculum.

Bennett's arguments against higher education are tightly connected:

First, colleges do not have the proper classical curriculum; second, they are wasteful, inefficient, and/or greedy. Certainty is the mother of efficiency; if you know the truth (the classical curriculum), the truth will make education free — or at least cheaper.

Bennett is one of the great educational theorists of the 19th century. His views are a tribute to his alma mater, Williams College, and its famous 19th-century president, Mark Hopkins. No less a person than James A. Garfield said that all you need for good education is "a student on one end of a log and Mark Hopkins on the other." Hopkins himself stated there was only one book needed in the library, the Bible.

Well, one book, one log, and one teacher make for pretty economical education. The 19th-century classical curriculum, fixed in content, direct in instruction, and sure in its moral assumptions, was a model of efficiency.

At the risk of being expelled from the University Presidents Mutual Protective Alliance, I have great sympathy with the secretary's urge to revive the classics, but the classical curriculum just won't do for the 20th — and 21st — century.

Somehow, Bennett has forgotten the rise of science, which played no role in the classical curriculum. If the classical curriculum delivered old truths, the scientific curriculum discovers new truths. Discovery is risky, uncertain, contentious, and "inefficient." Which line of research will discover the cure for cancer?

The modern college curriculum is not only scientific by addition, it is "scientific" throughout. We discover not only physical laws, but review our economic, political, artistic, and moral scholarship. Who knows, perhaps one day I may discover that Bill Bennett speaks great wisdom.

However, the secretary is correct: On the model of 19th-century collegiate education, modern universities are "inefficient." The fundamental issue is, do we want an educational delivery service or an instrument of discovery?

Identifying the Issues

With four essays on the same topic, you certainly get a lot of information. To identify the issues important to the topic, you need to look over your notes and make a list. If one essay raises the same issue as another, there is no point in listing it twice on this list, though later you will compare the sources' opinions on each issue. An initial list might look something like this:

Tuition has increased faster than inflation since 1980.
Tuition has not increased much more than inflation since 1970.
Reasons for increases not clear.
Financial aid has been cut.
Scientific curriculum costs more.

Equipment costs more.
Skilled professors cost money.
Government needs to give schools more support.
Higher tuition hurts students without money.
Schools have high costs for utilities, insurance, and so on.
More government support can lead to higher tuition.
Schools need to conserve on costs.

When you first list the issues, many of them will overlap because more than one source discusses the same issue. So you need to condense your list by grouping related items. For example, the first two issues deal with tuition increases compared with increases in the cost of living and inflation. Thus, you can define the more general issue as tuition versus inflation. Likewise, you can group all the reasons for higher tuition together under the more general issue of reasons. Other items show that financial aid is an important issue, and still others deal with funding—where money comes from to run universities. Grouping related issues into general topics, you might come up with a list like this:

Tuition versus inflation
Reasons for higher tuition
Financial aid
Funding

With a list this size you can begin to sort out how the author of each source feels about each issue. Each author will not necessarily comment on each issue, particularly if you are using many sources. Some authors may discuss only one or two of the issues. But by breaking down the issues, you can begin to see what your opinions are in contrast to the opinions of the authors. Here is one list you might create:

Tuition Versus Inflation
USA Today: Tuition has gone up only a little more than inflation since 1970.
Bennett: Tuition has gone up twice as much as inflation since 1980.
Your opinion: Tuition seems to have caught up with inflation since 1970. Now it should not go up more than inflation does.

Reasons for Higher Tuition
USA Today: Nobody seems to know, but catching up with inflation on salaries and building costs caused higher tuition and more expensive equipment such as computers.

Bennett: High financial aid lets colleges charge a lot; colleges need to "trim fat" from programs.

Hackney: In many fields professors have to get high salaries or they will work in industry rather than teach; universities have tried to cut costs, but operating costs, such as utilities and insurance, are up; also scientific equipment is expensive.

O'Brien: New scientific curriculum costs more than older classical curriculum, which he says Bennett favors.

Your opinion: Colleges should cut waste, but it is true that professors have to be paid well to stay in teaching, and new equipment raises costs.

Financial Aid
USA Today: Since 1980 there has been a large drop (68 to 37 percent) of students from families making less than $30,000, and students borrow more; financial aid cuts hurt students; aid needs to be increased.

Bennett: Higher financial aid contributes to higher tuition.

Hackney: Financial aid cuts have hurt students; students' opportunities should not be closed because of lack of money; colleges have had to provide more financial aid themselves.

Your opinion: Students who are needy and are willing to work hard in college deserve financial aid such as Pell grants. Also, they should not be denied loans as long as they will pay them back.

Funding
USA Today: Government and colleges need to work together on funding; government should not cut aid, and colleges should avoid wasteful spending.

Bennett: Colleges and universities need to do more to hold up "their end of the bargain."

Hackney: Colleges are following "cost-saving programs" and raising more money themselves; however, "federal aid is vital."

Your opinion: Colleges and government have to work together, maybe in some kind of program where the government helps schools by need but also gives a certain amount of money to a school that raises its own money.

Finding Your Thesis and Organizing Your Draft

Just as when you write in response to one or two sources, when writing a multiple-source essay you may find that your thesis and pattern of organization can change. Still, it is helpful to write a possible thesis and determine a pattern of organization to guide you as you draft.

Finding Your Thesis With a list of issues and notes on the sources' opinions and your own, you can begin to find where you stand on the topic. Look over the list and compare your opinions on each issue with the opinions of the sources. If necessary, go back and reread the sources if you are not clear about your opinion on an issue. Then go over the list of your opinions and try to write a sentence that expresses them generally. Remember that the thesis cannot mention each issue specifically, so try to develop a general but clear expression of your opinion. For example, the notes for your essay on college costs might lead to the following thesis:

> The government must work together with colleges and universities so all students who have the desire and ability to seek higher education can afford it.

This thesis, of course, cannot cover every opinion you expressed in your notes, but it allows you to get into the specifics of the issues in the body of the paper. There, you will expand on it, covering specific details about the need for working together to provide more financial aid, cutting wasteful spending, and meeting costs for new equipment and faculty salaries.

Organizing Your Draft As with any essay, you can write sections of your draft in any order you wish and arrange them later, or you can list the issues in the order you want to discuss them and then write the draft following that order. Remember that as you draft, you may discover a different purpose and thesis from the one you started with. Suppose you began drafting with the list of issues in the order presented earlier:

Tuition versus inflation
Reasons for higher tuition
Financial aid
Funding

This list would fit the thesis in the previous section because it suggests that you are defining a problem in the first three issues and then examining a solution in the last: how schools should be funded to minimize costs. However, if in writing you found that you were more interested in the hardships caused to students by cuts in financial aid, you could move that section to the end and discuss tuition versus inflation, reasons for high tuition, and funding problems as causes that create an undesirable effect on students. Thus, your purpose would change, and you would need to write a new thesis.

As you write your draft, remember to be flexible. If you start with a thesis and an arrangement of the issues, you might be able to follow it through. Remember, though, that the steps of the writing process overlap, so while drafting you may discover a thesis and a purpose that replace the ones you came up with in your original invention process. This can be frustrating, of course, but the writing process can be messy, as you learned in Chapter 1, and often our best ideas come as a result of writing.

■ Organizing Body Paragraphs in the Multiple-Source Essay

When you are writing about multiple sources, you are dealing with many issues and opinions. Thus, you need to take care that your paragraphs are focused and coherent. You can use any form of three-step method in the multiple-source essay, discussing one source in one paragraph and another source in another paragraph. However, at times you may want to discuss more than one source in a paragraph. Different versions of the three-step method can help.

Responding to Two Sources: The Three-Step Method

In the essay on hunting, you would probably want to make some direct comparisons of what Dunlap says and what Krutch says. You can use the three-step method from Chapter 4 by changing the questions a little.

1. What does the first source say?
2. What does the second source say?
3. What are your comments on the sources and why? Do you agree with both? disagree with both? agree with one and not the other? have mixed feelings on one? On both?

Answering the questions, in most cases, will enable you to write a coherent paragraph on a particular issue. Here are some examples.

>   (Step 1) Krutch argues that sport hunters destroy nature for no other reason than to "bring terror and agony" (35). (Step 2) Dunlap says that hunting — "which deals in death — can intensify our understanding of life," and he sees himself as a "brother animal" in a sometimes violent struggle with nature (13). (Step 3) Krutch may be exaggerating somewhat. Most sport hunters probably do not think of themselves the way he does. But they probably enjoy the power they feel in shooting an animal, and that is wrong. Dunlap sees hunting as more of a contest that helps us understand the idea of survival of the fittest and brings us closer to nature. But do we have to kill animals to understand nature? Can't hiking and camping bring us close to nature? Most hunters probably enjoy the thrill of the chase, but they should not glory in the idea of the violence as Dunlap does. Hunting for food is another way to use nature and must be done responsibly, but we should not enjoy killing animals or think of ourselves as animals.

  This paragraph expresses mixed feelings on both Krutch's and Dunlap's opinions of how hunters relate to nature. It then asserts the writer's opinion. By following the three steps, it sticks to and examines one issue in the debate on hunting.
  At other times you can discuss two sources that you agree with, expanding on their arguments.

(Step 1) The *USA Today* editorial points out that the percentage of students attending college from poor and lower-middle-class families dropped to 37 percent from 68 percent in 1980 (8a). (Step 2) Sheldon Hackney argues that "a student's abilities and interests, not financial status," should enable him or her to attend college (8a). (Step 3) These comments are right, for if the lower-income students can't afford to go to college, how can they advance in society? If college costs are beyond them, they will not have social mobility, which is one of the greatest promises of America. Without it, people lose hope and confidence in themselves and in their country.

Using the agreement between the sources as a starting point, the paragraph develops the issue of educational opportunities for students from low-income families.

At other times the sources might strongly disagree with each other, and you can follow with a discussion of your opinion on the issue.

(Step 1) Bennett claims that when the government raises financial aid, colleges and universities raise tuition because students with more aid can pay more (8a). (Step 2) In contrast, the *USA Today* editorial points out that student aid tripled in the 1970s when tuition costs were low compared with inflation, and as tuition costs have gone higher in the 1980s financial aid has been cut (8a). (Step 3) Bennett seems to be accusing schools of taking advantage of the government, but the figures from *USA Today* show that this is a false accusation. Some schools might do what Bennett says, but it would be foolish for schools to raise prices when aid is high because they could make tuition too expensive even for students who get financial aid. A school that tried to take advantage of the government and students this way would not be in business for long because students would go to schools where they can get their money's worth.

Responding to Three Sources: The Four-Step Method

This method is similar to the three-step method except that an additional question deals with the third source.

1. What does the first source say?
2. What does the second source say?
3. What does the third source say?
4. What are your comments on the sources and why? Do you agree with all three? disagree with all? agree with one and not the others? agree with two and not one? have mixed feelings on one? On two? On all?

Just as with the three-step method, your response to each source may vary. Thus, this method can produce many different kinds of paragraphs. Here is one example of how the four steps work.

(Step 1) Sheldon Hackney argues that "federal aid is vital" to help students reach their potential (8a). (Step 2) Similarly, the *USA Today* editorial calls for "liberal student loan programs, with strong payback provisions" (8a). (Step 3) William Bennett, however, says increased financial aid is not the answer to the high cost of education (8a). (Step 4) With lower financial aid, how does Bennett expect students to pay for college? Many already work part time, and the time spent working takes time from studying. Students can work and go to school, but if they work too many hours they cannot fulfill their potential, as Hackney says. I don't see anything wrong with increasing loans because if the program is run right to make sure people pay the loan back, the government actually makes money. It would not be hard to keep track of the loans by using a computer to identify borrowers when they file their income tax. If they have not paid that year, they could be forced to pay the loan along with their taxes. While loans should be increased, grants should continue for the needy and talented so that they do not spend the rest of their lives paying for college. Whatever the program, students need financial aid from the federal government.

This paragraph agrees with two of the sources, Hackney and *USA Today*, while disagreeing with Bennett. The four steps enable the writer to address the issue of financial aid in response to all three sources. The paragraph is a bit long, however. If you use the four-step method and find that the paragraph is too long to follow, you can break for a new paragraph as you begin step 4.

The Source Sandwich

Despite its odd name, the **source sandwich** can be an effective way to organize a body paragraph. Paragraphs using this method start with reference to a source, follow with the writer's comments, and end with reference to another source. Each source is like a piece of bread, and the writer's comments are the meat in the middle, as the following paragraph shows.

>   (Bread) Bennett claims that when the government raises financial aid, colleges and universities raise tuition prices because students with more aid can pay more (8a). (Meat) Bennett seems to be accusing schools of taking advantage of the government, but this is a false accusation. Some schools might do what Bennett says, but it would be foolish for schools to raise prices when aid is high because they could make tuition too expensive even for students who get financial aid. A school that tried to take advantage of the government and students this way would not be in business for long because students would go to schools where they can get their money's worth. (Bread) As the *USA Today* editorial points out, student aid tripled in the 1970s when tuition costs were low compared with inflation, and as tuition costs have gone higher in the 1980s financial aid has been cut (8a).

You probably recognize much of the information in this paragraph because it is similar to the version illustrating the three-step method. In this paragraph, however, the second source has been moved to the end of the paragraph where it still denies Bennett's claim and backs up the writer's. You can also use the source sandwich with three sources, putting two first and one last, or vice versa, depending on your purpose.

>   (Bread) Dennis O'Brien, president of the University of Rochester, points out that increases in scientific education have

Writing the Multiple-Source Essay

contributed to the high cost of education (8a). Likewise, Sheldon Hackney mentions the costs of technological equipment and salaries for professors in fields where they could earn a great deal in private industry (8a). (Meat) Education certainly costs more these days. Just a few years ago, a school did not have to worry about budgeting money for computers. But today, most schools have computer labs for everything from physics to writing. Also, as other equipment becomes more advanced, it costs more, but without it students can't learn the most current knowledge. (Bread) Thus, William Bennett is wrong to say that schools should not point to the increased cost of knowledge to justify higher tuition (8a).

All of the methods for organizing body paragraphs allow you to discuss two or three sources. Until you gain more experience writing source essays, you probably should not try to deal with more than three sources in a paragraph. And even experienced writers rarely discuss more than two or three because too many sources in a paragraph can cause the reader to get confused and will not leave much room for the writer's comments. Your comments are the most important part of the essay.

As you gain experience, you will find additional ways to organize according to your purpose and depending on the sources. Remember that even in a multiple-source essay, you can use the simple three-step method dealing with one source at a time if that seems the best way to organize the essay. You can also raise issues not mentioned in the sources, so that some of your paragraphs might not refer to the sources at all. The methods considered here may not cover every situation or solve all your organizational problems, but they can help make your paragraphs more coherent if you use them in planning, writing, and revising your drafts.

■ Writing an Introduction to a Multiple-Source Essay

Like any introduction, the introduction to the multiple-source essay should get the reader's attention, introduce and limit the topic, and state your thesis. Chapter 4 presented two types of introductions for single-source essays: opening summary, and introductory strategy and summary. These two can work for some multiple-source essays. A third type draws on some of the strategies you learned in Chapter 1.

Opening Summary

In the single-source essay, this method includes a summary of the source's essay and a statement of your thesis. You can use the same technique in writing about two or three or even four sources, as long as you keep the summaries brief.

> In *The Great Chain of Life,* Joseph Wood Krutch argues that hunters who kill animals just for sport are doing the worst kind of evil. He also questions the morality of people who hunt for food, though he admits they have a purpose. John C. Dunlap, author of "In Defense of Hunting," asks why people do not hunt, and he goes on to argue that hunting is no different from eating food from a supermarket, that it contributes to game management, and that it helps people understand nature. Hunting purely for sport is brutal, but not all hunting is a form of brutality.
>
> A recent issue of *USA Today* printed an editorial and three guest columns debating the causes and effects of increases in college tuition. The editorial criticized colleges for higher costs but also recommended that the government increase financial aid. Sheldon Hackney, president of the University of Pennsylvania, defended colleges, arguing that they are trying to save money but that higher costs for teachers and equipment lead to higher tuition. He also contended that federal aid should be increased. Dennis O'Brien, University of Rochester president, said higher costs were the result of scientific education. In contrast, Secretary of Education William Bennett said colleges waste money and raise tuition whenever financial aid goes up. Education is crucial to America. Instead of arguing about tuition costs, the government should work together with colleges and universities so that all students who have the desire and ability to seek higher education can afford it.

In both introductions, the summaries are short, in some cases only one sentence stating the author's thesis. Sometimes you may have to reduce a whole book to one sentence. The summary introduction works best only if you have a small number of sources.

Introductory Strategy and Opening Summary

All the strategies you learned in Chapter 1 can be used to get the reader's attention and define the topic before you move to your summary and thesis. Depending on the length of the strategy and the summary, however, you may need to extend the introduction to two paragraphs. Compare the following introductions.

Opening Question: One Paragraph

Is a man who kills his limit during deer season and then butchers and freezes the meat so his family has food the same as a man who shoots a lion on a safari, mounts the head in his office, uses the skin for a throw rug in front of a fireplace, but has no taste or use for the meat? In his essay about killing for sport, Joseph Wood Krutch argues that hunters who kill animals just for sport are doing the worst kind of evil. He also questions the morality of people who hunt for food, though he admits they have a purpose. John C. Dunlap, author of "In Defense of Hunting," asks why people do not hunt, and he goes on to argue that hunting is no different from eating food from a supermarket, that it contributes to game management, and that it helps people understand nature. Hunting purely for sport is brutal, but not all hunting is a form of brutality.

Narrating: Two Paragraphs

Anthony Washburn entered a prestigious eastern university last fall, quite an accomplishment for a young black man from a single-parent home in Nashville, Tennessee. With a private scholarship, a government Pell grant, earnings from a part-time job, and what little his mother could contribute, he managed to pay his tuition, buy his books, and have a little pocket change. Anthony is back in Nashville this fall. No, he didn't flunk out. But when tuition increased $1500 and the government decided his private scholarships disqualified him from the Pell grant, Anthony had to defer his dream. Now he is working full time, taking evening classes at a local state university, and hoping to earn enough money to return east next fall. These days, we hear about students like Anthony all too often.

A recent issue of *USA Today* printed an editorial and three guest columns debating the causes and effects of increases in college tuition. The editorial criticized colleges for higher costs but also recommended that the government increase financial aid. Sheldon Hackney, president of the University of Pennsylvania, defended colleges, arguing that colleges are trying to save money but that higher costs for teachers and equipment lead to higher tuition. He also contended that federal aid should be increased. Dennis O'Brien, University of Rochester president, said higher costs were the result of scientific education. In contrast, Secretary of Education William Bennett said colleges waste money and raise tuition whenever financial aid goes up. Education is crucial to America. Instead of arguing about tuition costs, the government should work together with colleges and universities so that all students who have the desire and ability to seek higher education can afford it.

The first of these introductions is very much like the example in the last chapter: it adds the question strategy, but now there is a summary of Dunlap's essay along with the summary of Krutch's. The second uses narration (the story about Anthony Washburn) to involve the reader, to add human interest before getting to the topic. Because of the length of the narration, the summary and thesis must follow in a second paragraph. An introduction of this sort is more appropriate to a longer paper. You wouldn't want an introduction of two paragraphs if the whole essay is only five or six paragraphs.

Introductory Strategy Without Direct Reference to the Sources

If you are writing on a topic and read five, six, or more sources, you cannot summarize all of them in the introduction because by the time you get to your thesis, you will have lost the reader's attention. When you have many sources, it is best just to use one of the introductory strategies to define and limit the topic and state your thesis. Any of the strategies studied in Chapter 1 would work. For instance, you could add the thesis on the cost of education to the narration about Anthony and use that paragraph as an introduction. Then you could discuss the sources only in the body paragraphs. Using the sources only in the body is fine as long as the introduction has done the job of introducing your topic and stating your thesis.

Another way to handle several sources in the introduction is to write one or two sentences saying that several authors have been concerned with the topic and have written on it. Note the italicized sentence in the following introduction:

> A popular slogan of people who support increased funds for education reads, "If you think education is expensive, try the cost of ignorance." Any student or parent today knows the cost of higher education. Tuition, which has risen dramatically in the last few years, is only one part of the cost of pursuing a degree. Books, supplies, incidentals, and, for many students, living costs can double the price. *Several educators and authorities have attempted to find the causes and propose solutions to the rising costs of higher education, but no one has the answer.* With many students facing the cost of ignorance, the government should work together with colleges and universities so that all students who have the desire and ability to seek higher education can afford it.

Using the opening quotation, this is a standard introduction, but the italicized sentence lets the reader know that you have been reading about the topic and that the essay will more than likely refer to some of the educators and authorities for support. Thus, the reader is prepared for the body paragraphs that follow.

■ Writing a Conclusion to a Multiple-Source Essay

Just as in any essay, the conclusion for a multiple-source essay has the following purposes: to stress the thesis, to leave an impression, and to give the essay a sense of completeness. You can use any of the strategies you learned in Chapter 1. As in the single-source essay, you should try to refer to the sources in the conclusion if you are writing about two or three sources.

> Krutch is right to say that "killing for killing's sake is a terrifying phenomenon" (35). However, Dunlap's arguments about the laws of nature and the purpose of game management show that not all hunters kill for the sake of killing. People have hunted since the beginning of time, and though hunting is associated with uncivilized societies, hunters can be civilized if, along with their guns, they take responsibility and respect for nature into the woods.

Working the sources into such a conclusion is not difficult because there are only two. However, when you have many sources, you cannot refer to all of them in the conclusion. You can either use a concluding strategy without reference to the sources or pick a particularly strong quote from one source and work it in, as in the following examples.

No Reference to the Sources

> University administrators and government officials must find a way to keep college affordable without sacrificing the quality of education. Money should not stand between students and their desire to develop themselves to their fullest potential. Ask Anthony Washburn.

You may recognize this strategy from Chapter 1, where it was called "echoing the introduction." While the thesis is echoed in the first two sentences, the reference to Anthony returns the reader to the human interest element that began the essay. While this conclusion is effective, a quotation from one source could work as well:

> University administrators and government officials must find a way to keep college affordable without sacrificing the quality of education. Money should not stand between students and their desire to develop themselves to their fullest potential. As the *USA Today* editorial put it, "You don't need a college degree to know something's wrong here" (8a).

Writing the Multiple-Source Essay   139

■ Revising and Editing Checklists for the Multiple-Source Essay

Many of the concerns you will have in revising and editing the multiple-source essay are similar to those that apply to the single-source essay and, for that matter, to all essays. The following checklists can guide your revision and editing.

Revising

1. Does your introduction make it clear that you will be drawing on multiple sources?
2. Each time you cite a source for the first time, do you use the author's full name?
3. Are the source's points clearly tagged so that the reader can tell them from your own?
4. Does the essay refer to the sources at various points so that it avoids drifting off into a personal essay?
5. Do you present the sources' ideas accurately and clearly when you paraphrase them?
6. Do you use your own words and sentence structure when you paraphrase?
7. Do your responses logically follow from or lead to the sources' ideas? In other words, are you and the sources talking about the same issue?
8. When you are discussing more than one source at a time, is the position of each source clear?
9. If you use the three-step method, are all steps clear and is step 3 fully developed?
10. Do your body paragraphs end in agreement with your thesis?
11. Does your conclusion reassert your thesis?

Editing

1. If a source is a book, have you underlined the title?
2. If a source is an essay, have you placed the title in quotation marks?
3. If you have quoted the sources, have you used their *exact* words?
4. If you have left words out of a quotation, have you used ellipsis points?
5. In integrating quotations, have you avoided sentence errors such as comma splices and run-on sentences?
6. Have you cited sources with parenthetical citation (page numbers in parentheses)?
7. Have you used the proper forms for entering the sources on your list of works cited?

Credits

William J. Bennett, "Taxpayer Subsidies Help Fuel Tuition Hikes," reprinted courtesy of William J. Bennett, from *USA Today,* 1987.

Excerpt from *America Past and Present,* Robert A. Divine, et al., p. 940. Copyright © 1987, 1984 by Scott, Foresman and Company. HarperCollins College Publishers.

John C. Dunlap, "In Defense of Hunting," from *Newsweek,* 1983.

Joseph Wood Krutch, from *The Great Chain of Life* by Joseph Wood Krutch. Copyright © 1956 by Joseph Wood Krutch. Copyright © renewed 1984 by Marcelle L. Krutch. Reprinted by permission of Houghton Mifflin Company. All rights reserved.

Sheldon Hackney, "Colleges Must Not Cut Quality to Curb Costs," reprinted courtesy of Sheldon Hackney, from *USA Today,* 1987.

William Morris, Editor, Entry for "effect," from *The American Heritage Dictionary of the English Language.* Copyright © 1981 by Houghton Mifflin Company. Reprinted by permission from *The American Heritage Dictionary of the English Language.*

Dennis O'Brien, "It's Simply Classical Economics," reprinted courtesy of Dennis O'Brien, from *USA Today,* 1987.

USA Today, "Colleges Must Cut Costs, Help Students." Copyright 1987, *USA Today.* Reprinted with permission.

Excerpt from *Psychology and Life,* 11th ed. by Philip G. Zimbardo, p. 471. Copyright © 1985, 1979, 1977, 1975 by Scott, Foresman and Company. HarperCollins College Publishers.

Index

Active reading, 42–43, 59
Agreeing with source in single-source essay
   three-step method in, 97–101
   three-step method turned upside down in, 101–103
Alternating coverage as essay strategy, 23–24
The American Heritage Dictionary of the English Language, 54–58
Analyzing causes as essay strategy, 21–22
Annotating of texts, 58–61
Argumentative thesis, 11
Asking questions in essay introductions, 33–34. *See also* Questions
Audience
   essay, 3, 11–13
   revising for, 17

Bennett's "Taxpayer Subsidies Help Fuel Tuition Hikes," 123–124
Block quotations, 78–80

Body paragraph organization
   multiple-source essay and, 129–134
   single-source essay and, 97–104
Books
   essays in, 84–85
   with one author, 83
   with several authors, 83–84
   sources in, 66
Brackets
   key words or phrases and, 59, 63
   quotations and square, 81
Brainstorming
   essays and, 6–7
   single-source, 92–93
Built-in qualities in classifying, 25
but, 99

Catchy language, 73
cf. (confer), 61
Challenging reader in concluding paragraph, 38

143

Checklists
  in revising and editing
    of multiple source essay, 140–141
    of single-source essay, 109–110
Chronological order as essay strategy, 18–19
Classification as essay strategy, 17, 18, 24–25
Cluster diagram, 8
Clustering
  reading and, 63–64
  writing process and, 7
College costs, essays on, 119–125
"Colleges Must Cut Costs, Help Students," 120–121
"Colleges Must Not Cut Quality to Curb Costs," 121–123
Colon introducing quoted sentence, 77–78
compare (cp.), 61
Comparing and contrasting as essay strategy, 17, 22–24
  multiple sources in, 111–116. *See also* Multiple-source essay
Comprehension, 43–61
  annotating texts in, 58–61
  frame of reference and context in, 44–45
  main ideas in, 45–51
  unknown words in, 51–58
Conclusion
  challenging reader in, 38
  looking to future in, 39
  to multiple-source essay, 138–139
  paragraph, 28, 36–40
    purpose and quality of, 36–37
    problem solving of, 37–38
  to single-source essay, 108–109
confer (cf.), 61
Consecutive words, paraphrasing and, 72
Context
  and frame of reference, 44–45
  guessing from, 51–53
  reading and, 51–53
Contrast
  as essay strategy, 17, 22–24
  multiple sources and, 111–116. *See also* Multiple-source essay
cp. (compare), 61

Cross-references
  dictionary and, 55, 57
  marginal note and, 61
  reading and, 61

"In Defense of Hunting," 110–114
Defining as essay strategy, 25–26
Definitions, dictionary and, 54–58
Demonstrable thesis, 11
Descriptive introduction, 32
Development
  draft, for essays, 14–15. *See also* Draft
  paragraph, 97–104
  revising essays for, 16
Dictionary usage, 53–58
Disagreeing with source in single-source essay
  three-step method in, 98–99
  three-step method upside down in, 102
Documenting of sources, 82
Draft
  development of, 14–15
  organizing of, 13–14
    multiple-source essay and, 118–119, 129
    single-source essay and, 95–96
  revising of, 15–17
Dunlap's "In Defense of Hunting," 110–114

Echoing of introduction in concluding paragraph, 38
Editing, checklists for, 109–110, 140–141
Editorials
  on college costs, 119–125
Effect, causes and, 21
Ellipsis points in quotations, 80–81
Entry in list of works cited, 82
Essay process. *See also* Essays; Writing essays
  audience in, 11–13
  drafting of essay in, 13–15
  finding topic in, 5
  invention strategies for topic in, 6–9
  revising drafts in, 15–17
  thesis sentence in, 9–11
Essays, 1–40. *See also* Essay process
  in book, 84–85
  classification in, 17, 18, 24–25
  comparison-contrast. *See* Comparing

144   Index

and contrasting as essay strategy;
    Multiple-source essay
  conclusion of, 36–40
  draft of. *See* Draft
  introduction to. *See* Introduction
  length of, 22
  mixing strategies in, 26–28
  multiple-source, 111–141. *See also*
    Multiple-source essay
  organization of. *See* Organization
  paragraphs and, 2
  single-source, 88–110. *See also* Single-
    source essay
  strategies for. *See* Essay strategies
  thesis for, 4
  topics for, 3–4
  writing process for. *See* Writing essays
Essay strategies, 17–28
  analyzing causes in, 21–22
  analyzing a process in, 19–21
  classifying in, 24–25
  comparing and contrasting in, 22–24
  defining in, 25–26
  narrating in, 18–19
Etymology, 55, 57

Frame of reference, 44–45
Freewriting, 8

General thesis sentence, 4
"The Great Chain of Life," 91–92
Guessing from context, 51–53

Hackney's "Colleges Must Not Cut
    Quality to Curb Costs," 121–123
however, 99

Identifying issues, 115, 125–128
Implied ideas, 48–50
imply, 49
Imposed qualities in classifying, 25
Interviews, sources in, 67–68, 86–87
Introduction, 28–36
  descriptive, 32
  echoing of, in concluding paragraph, 38
  to multiple-source essay, 134–138
  purpose of, 30
  questions in, 33–34
  to single-source essay, 104–108

Introductory paragraph, 28–36. *See also*
    Introduction
Invention. *See also* Invention strategies
  free writing as strategy for, 55
  multiple-source essay and, 114
  single-source essay and, 90–93
Invention strategies. *See also* Invention
  topic and, 6–9
Issues
  comparing and contrasting sources
    and, 111–116. *See also* Multiple-
    source essay
  identifying, 125–128
  not in source, 102
  "It's Simply Classical Economics," 124–125

Journalist questions, 7

Key words, paraphrasing and, 72–73
Krutch's "The Great Chain of Life," 91–92

Language, striking or catchy, 73
Length
  of essay, 2
  of summary, 74–75
Lists, of works cited, 82–87

Magazines, sources in, 67, 85
Main idea, 45–51. *See also* Thesis
  delayed, 47
  first, 46–47
  implied, 48–50
  last, 47–48
  split, 50–51
Major causes as essay strategy, 21–22
Marginal notes, 60–61
Meanings
  dictionary and, 54
  reading and, 42
  responding to, 43
Mechanics of writing, 65–87. *See also*
    Sources
Minor causes as essay strategy, 21–22
Mixed response, single-source essay
    and, 99–100
Mixing strategies in essays, 26–28
Multiple-source essay, 211–241
  conclusion to, 138–139
  four-step method in, 131–133

Multiple-source essay (*cont.*)
   introduction to, 134–138
   organizing body paragraphs in, 129–134
   responding to three or more sources in, 119–129
   responding to two sources in, 111–119
   revising and editing checklists for, 140–141

Narrating
   as essay strategy, 18–19
   introduction to single-source essay and, 106–107
   thesis introduction and, 31–32
nevertheless, 99
Newspapers as sources, 66, 86
Notes, marginal, 60–61

O'Brien's "It's Simply Classical Economics," 124–125
on the other hand, 99
Opening summary
   multiple-source essay and, 135–137
   single-source essay and, 105–108
Opinions, comparing and contrasting sources and, 115–116. *See also* Multiple-source essay
Organization
   body paragraph, 97–104
      multiple-source essay and, 129–134
   draft, 13–15
   invention notes and, 13
   multiple-source essay and, 118–119
   revision and, 16
   single-source essay and, 95–96

Paragraphs, 2, 28–40
   body
      multiple-source essay and, 129–134
      single-source essay and, 97–104
   conclusion and, 28, 36–40
   essays compared to, 2
   introduction of, 28–36
      funnel, 31
   introductions and conclusions, 28–40
      conclusions in, 36–40
      introductions in, 28–30
   without reference to source in single-source essay, 103–104
Paraphrasing, 69–73
   steps of, 70–71
   using own words in, 71–73
Parenthetical citation, 73
Pattern of organization. *See* Organization
Person
   introducing thesis by describing, 32
Place, description of, 32
Plagiarism, 68–69
Posing questions. *See* Questions
Problem solving, essay conclusion and, 37–38
Process, writing essay. *See* Writing essays
Process analysis in essay writing, 19–21
Product of essay, 1–5
Pronunciation key, 54, 55–56
Purpose
   of source in single-source essay, 89–90
   thesis in single-source essay and, 94–95
   of writer of essay, 2

Questions
   essay conclusion and, 39, 39–40
   essay introduction and, 34
      single-source, 107
   journalist, 7, 15
Quotation marks, 76
Quotations, 75–82
   block, 78–80
   in essay introduction, 35
   strategies for, 75–82
   tags in, 76

Reader
   challenging, 38
   shocking and surprising, 33
Reading, 41–64
   active, 42–43, 59
   comprehension of, 43–61
      annotating texts in, 58–61
      frame of reference and context in, 44–45
      picking out main ideas in, 45–51
      unknown words in, 51–58
   meaning in, 42–43
   speed, 61–64
Reading responses, 43
Reference
   cross, 55, 57
   frame of, 44–45

list of works cited and, 82
in paragraph introduction, 35–36
Revision
  for audience, 17
  checklist, 109–110
    multiple-source essay and, 140–141
  for development, 16
  draft, 15–17
  for organization, 16
  thesis, 15–16

Scholarly journals as sources, 67
Selecting
  in single-source essay introduction, 105–106
  in thesis introduction, 31
Sentence thesis, 9–11
  thesis in, 4, 9–11
Series of questions in essay introduction, 33–34
Shocking statements, 34
Single-source essay, 88–110
  conclusion of, 108–109
  introduction to, 104–108
  invention in, 90–91
  organizing in
    developing body paragraphs and, 97–104
    drafting and, 95–96
  purpose of source in, 89–90
  purpose and thesis in, 94–95
  revising and editing checklists in, 109–110
  three-step method in, 97–101
  upside down, 101–104
Skimming in reading, 62–63
Solving of problem in essay conclusion, 37–38
Sources, 65–87
  agreeing with
    three-step method in, 97–98
    three-step method turned upside down in, 101–102
  documenting, 82
  list of works cited in, 82–87
  multiple. *See* Multiple-source essay
  paraphrasing in, 69–73
  purpose of, single-source essay and, 89–90
  quotations from, 75–82
  summarizing and, 74–75
  types of, 65–69

Source sandwich, 133
Speed reading, 61–64
  comprehension and, 61
Spelling, dictionary and, 54
Square brackets, 81
Strategies. *See* Essay strategies.
Striking language, paraphrasing and, 73
Subjects, essay, 3–4, 5. *See also* Thesis; Topic essay, invention strategies and
Successive coverage as essay strategy, 23
Summary, 74–75
  length of, 74–75
  multiple-source essay opening, 135–136
    introductory strategy in, 137–138
  purpose of, 74–75
  single-source essay opening, 104–105
    introductory strategy in, 105–108
Summary note in reading, 60–61
Surprising statement
  example of, 34
  in introduction
    to paragraph, 34
    to single-source essay, 107–108
Syllables, 54, 55
Synonyms, 55, 57
  paraphrasing and, 72

Tag
  in paraphrase, 71
  in quotation, 76
"Taxpayer Subsidies Help Fuel Tuition Hikes," 123–124
Text annotation, 58–61
that, 79
Thesis, 4, 9–11. *See also* Main idea
  argumentative or demonstrable, 11
  description of, 10–11
  general or specific sentence for, 10–11
  limited, 10
  multiple-source essay, 116–119, 128–129
  revision of, 15–16
  single-source essay, 104–108
    finding purpose in, 89–90
    introductory strategy for summary in, 105

Index 147

Three-step method
  body paragraph organization by, 97–101
  upside down, 101–103
  multiple-source essay and, 130–131
Topic, essay, 3–4, 5
  invention strategies and, 6–9
Two sources, responding to, 130–131.
  See also Multiple-source essay

Underlining in paragraph, 59
Unknown words in reading, 51–58
USA Today editorial "Colleges Must Cut Costs, Help Students," 120–121

Words
  spelling of, 54
  strategies for using own, 71
  syllables of, 54, 55
  unknown, 51–58
Works cited in list, 82–87
Writer, purpose of, essays and, 2
Writing of essays. *See* Writing essays

Writing essays
  process of, 5–17
    audience in, 11–13
    drafting in, 13–15
    finding topic in, 5
    invention strategies to find topic in, 6–9
    organizing invention notes in, 13
    revising drafts in, 15–17
    thesis sentence in, 9–11
  product in, 1–5
  strategy of, 17–28
    analyzing causes in, 21–22
    analyzing process in, 19–21
    classifying in, 24–25
    comparing and contrasting in, 22–24
    defining in, 25–26
    mixing in, 26–28
Writing situation, process analysis and, 19–21

Yes/no note in margin of text, 60

A Note to Instructors

You've probably been hearing students complain about the price of textbooks for quite some time now. Perhaps you or your colleagues, concerned with the rising costs of education, have voiced similar complaints yourselves. As one of this country's leading educational publishers, we felt it was time to address those concerns.

The textbook you hold in your hands represents a bold new initiative for this discipline. HarperCollins (and other publishers) have issued compact texts and brief versions of full-length texts before. But now, for the first time, we're creating a complete series of related brief texts, carefully conceived to stand alone or mesh seamlessly together. You can choose one, or several, depending on your course needs; use them as core texts or supplemental material.

And though they're brief, they're of the highest quality — comprehensive, practical, well written. So while you're saving your students money, you're not shortchanging them on educational value.

Another thing you may notice about these texts is the student-oriented packaging strategy. We felt that no matter how good they are, or how much of a value they represent, all your concern and our effort is for naught if students don't actually *buy* the books. So we've employed catchy teasers to entice browsing students to read the back covers, where we point out that the books are short on price and long on utility. We hope that they'll recognize the favor you've done them, and strongly consider purchasing the books instead of sharing or doing without. We feel that once you have urged students to buy a particular book for your course, you've done your part; we want to follow up by maximizing the chances that they'll come to your class with the book in their bag.

Thank you for looking into this new, value-priced series from HarperCollins. We appreciate your concerns, and trust that we've responded thoughtfully and effectively. We hope this is an option you'll welcome.